Forgetta 'bout It

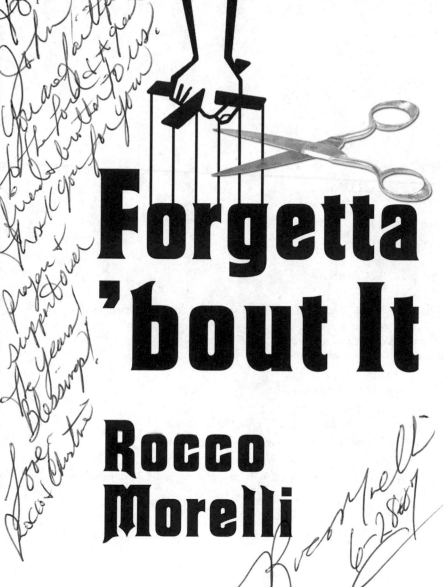

Forgetta 'bout It

Rocco Morelli

From Mafia to Ministry

Bridge-Logos
Orlando, Florida 32822

Bridge-Logos

Orlando, FL 32822 USA

Forgetta 'bout It'
by Rocco Morelli

Copyright ©2007 by Bridge-Logos

Printed in the United States of America.

Library of Congress Catalog Card Number: 2006940408
International Standard Book Number 978-0-88270-323-7

Scripture quotations in this book are from the *King James Version* of the Bible.

G.163.316.N.m701.35250

Dedication

This book is dedicated to the lost and hurting people all around this world. "You are not forgotten!"

To my parents, Hugo and Mary whose unconditional love and prayers prevailed. "Thank you for never giving up on me!"

To my daughter Racquel who is now a grown woman but will always be "Daddy's Girl."

And most of all to my lovely wife Christine who has blessed my life. "Baby, you're the best!"

I love you all very much and most of all I love God and thank Him for rescuing me right on time.

As Marvis Frazier, former boxer and son of Smokin' Joe Frazier (heavy weight champion of the world) says, "I am blessed by the Best, sharing it with the rest!"

Contents

Foreword

I first met Rocco Morelli at an altar call at a Full Gospel Businessmen's dinner in New Kensington, Pennsylvania— a city known by many as "Little Chicago."

I was the guest speaker sharing about the love and forgiveness of Jesus Christ. Standing in front of my wife Dorothy and myself asking for prayer was a young heartbroken husband and father who was waiting to be sentenced to prison for his crimes.

Rocco had two things in his favor: A strong Italian father who loved him and a precious mother who knew how to touch the heart of God for her only son.

This book is about a young man who once thought he had the world in his hands until he met Jesus of Nazareth and finally came to realize what he had wasn't enough. Jesus not only forgave him for all his sins, but also led him out of darkness into His marvelous light.

"For what profit is it to a man if he gains the whole world and loses his own soul?" (Matthew 16:26)

Stephen Totin
Prison Coordinator
Cornerstone Television
Wall, Pennsylvania

Introduction

This is my story: Rocco Morelli—cop, politician, heir to the mob. A Mafia wise guy.

I became rich, powerful, and greedy. I was arrested and imprisoned. But I reformed, and when released from prison, was a changed man—from Mafia to ministry.

La famiglia (the family) ran "Little Chicago," the nickname of my hometown of New Kensington, Pennsylvania, so-called because of its mob connections.

Frank Sinatra and his famous rat pack (Dean Martin, Peter Lawford, Joey Bishop, and Sammy Davis, Jr.) were frequent visitors to our notorious city, along with many other celebrities. Mafia bosses on the east coast all had ties to the family in Little Chicago.

The Mafia curse was passed down to me from my great-grandfather. I was doomed from birth to be an heir of the mob. I was power-hungry and wanted it all. I kept my feet in both worlds—the legitimate and illegitimate—while involved in mob activities. I became a cop at age nineteen, while maintaining my love for the underworld.

I was a business entrepreneur with my hand in politics while working on my wiseguy career. As I learned about the "Pizza Connection," I became a player and eventually messed up my mind with a potent mix of drugs and alcohol.

Less than ten years later I had the world in the palm of my hands. I was part of the action and made my moves to become a made-man in the mob. My friend and right-hand man turned out to be a snitch. The boss gave me the opportunity for membership. "Kill Tony and you're made!" All I needed was an ironclad alibi.

As I was about to do the hit, something happened that changed my plans and my life forever. Something that made all the difference in the world.

This book should appeal to Christians and everyone who is drawn to Mafia stories. It can be introduced as approved reading material for every prison library and chapel in the United States and internationally as well.

Chapter 1

The "Rock"

I was the "chosen one." As my grandfather's namesake, the only male offspring, I alone would carry on the Morelli name.

Was this a glorious inheritance, or a curse?

When I was a bambino, my great-aunt performed a traditional Italian ritual on me. She concluded that someone had given me "the evil eye" at birth, and I was cursed.

My Aunt Assunta and Uncle Peppino had moved from Italy to Venezuela in South America several years before. My grandfather brought them to the U.S. back in 1960, right after I was born.

Aunt Assunta became concerned at how I howled and cried whenever I was brought to my grandparents' home. One day, she took me in her arms and prayed to remove the *maluche*, the name the Italians gave to a curse of the devil.

Perhaps because of that "curse," I always had to fight my way to the top, especially to become someone who people respected and ultimately feared.

When I was five years old, the neighborhood bullies picked on me big time. One kid always called me "Rockhead" and "Stone," cursing at me and throwing rocks at my head as he rode his bike past my house.

One day I started throwing rocks back. That only escalated the situation. Finally, I decided I had enough. I ran after him, knocked him off his bike and began punching him. I hit him with everything I had. One punch broke his nose, and blood splattered everywhere. He retreated. I was now the "Champ." No one would ever knock the Rock again.

The rest of the gang shook my hand and later he did too. He said he was sorry and asked me to be part of the gang. I accepted and apologized for hitting him so hard. Frankly, I really enjoyed my victory.

I decided that no one would ever make me look like a jerk again. If anyone hurt me, I would hurt them back even more. Vengeance was always sweet in those days. My mantra was a verse written in the Old Testament: "An eye for an eye, a tooth for a tooth."

When I went into the first grade attending Catholic school, I was somewhat fearful of all the other kids. But one thing that was in my favor was that the neighborhood bully was now my friend and was in my grade. The downside was that I had to become tough enough to defend my new challengers.

Fighting for my honor only got worse, and I had to pretend to like it. The *Rocky* movie didn't help matters. I had to live up to the "Italian Stallion," else I would have been jerked around the rest of my life.

I actually hated fighting. I especially hated to get hit. I had to protect my "pretty boy face," and God forbid you should mess up my fancy duds or perfect hairdo.

I learned how to duck and hit quick and fast to take out my opponent. I learned how to neutralize a better fighter or more than one opponent. A blackjack to the head always seemed to work.

By high school I had a reputation of being a playboy, musician, and junior wise guy. I kept a switchblade in my glove box, a club under my seat and a loaded 12-gauge shotgun in my trunk. Many came to know the wrath of Rocco. While most of my classmates were being studious, I practiced being devious.

I became street smart and an intellectual genius. Making the transition from Catholic school to a public high school was a piece of cake. I was so far advanced academically in Catholic school that I never took a book home to study in high school.

My mind went beyond the boredom of school subjects. My extracurricular activities consisted of skipping school to hang out with other "wise guys" and learn every vice, scheme, and trick in the underworld of "big money business."

Another name for this is "racketeering."

The hustle was where it was. I wanted to be in on the "action." I wasn't great at the pool hustle so I became focused on playing cards. I learned every trick and that the hand must be quicker than the eye. You also have to have a great mind and memory for the game.

I started playing poker and blackjack when I was eight. My uncle Eddie was a good teacher. He even took me to horse and Greyhound dog racing, taught me how to read a racing form and calculate the odds to wager bets on the ponies and dogs. At age fifteen I was a player with the big boys. It became an obsession just like my first drink, the first joint I smoked, the line of cocaine I snorted, or the pills I swallowed to make me feel good. I always wanted more.

I manipulated my parents, teachers, business people, my friends and peers—anyone who would listen to my convincing and compelling stories to further my cause to fame and fortune.

Even as a young boy, I had the ability to charm my way through life. People always seemed to like me and were drawn by my charisma.

It was cute during my years of innocence. It became a tool of power and manipulation as I came of age. I learned that I could talk my way out of most anything. My charm, good looks and convincing dialogue could've qualified me for an Academy Award.

I had severe health problems growing up, which covered up my tracks of absenteeism. I suffered from chronic allergies that required ongoing treatment and ever restricted my activities. I was pretty much given a permanent "hall pass."

I used my disability to enhance my abilities in organized crime. I enterprised my criminal activities to bookmaking, selling drugs, and "hot" merchandise. I became what was known as a "fence," or a dealer in stolen property. I was also a loan shark, professional gambler, and bookmaker, taking illegal bets.

I was exercising entrepreneurship as a capitalist in the free world. What could possibly be wrong with that? This is America, the land of opportunity. The world could be mine if I wanted it bad enough.

You could have literally bought anything your heart desired from me in those days and in the years that followed. If you needed a date, I could even arrange that, for a price of course. Nothing was free unless I liked you and wanted to give you something.

I started having a lot of friends. Now I was the man, the "Rock."

At age fifteen, I forged a birth certificate to get my driver's license because I didn't want to wait another year. I eventually got caught because I bragged about it.

My dad helped me to get out of it, though, and I told a little white lie to the judge, and he let me off the hook. It was all prearranged through the family.

I also got my Musicians' Union card at fifteen and drank in every joint where we performed and was never asked for identification until I was twenty-one and celebrating my birthday. The bar owner asked what the party was about. I told her that I had finally turned twenty-one. She almost fell over.

She gave me a drink on the house and said, "What the heck … you looked old enough to me all those years."

My success at deception paved the way for my life in organized crime.

You name it, I did it. I was the man, the Little Prince of Little Chicago.

Chapter 2

The "Young Prince"

When I was young I became an altar boy in Mt. St. Peter Catholic Church. It was an honor and also expected of good boys from the better families.

I had been baptized into the Roman Catholic Church as an infant. As a small boy, I went through catechism classes, memorizing the secrets and mysteries of God and His relationship to man. As a little guy, I knelt with all the other kids in my class and received my First Communion.

I had no choice about it. I was born a Christian. My family was Christian. When we did wrong, we went to confession. There, we bared everything sinful in our lives to Almighty God and our parish priest, who was obligated by 2,000 years of Church rules to assure us of God's forgiveness and to keep to himself our confessed evil. Priests have died refusing to divulge what was told them in the confidentiality of confession.

But was I a Christian? Did I earn God's forgiveness by doing the penance assigned me—reciting The Lord's Prayer over and over for lying to my mother, or doing multiple rosaries for stealing a cookie?

As a good Catholic boy, I thought so. I confessed everything. And I received forgiveness.

But was I a Christian?

I had a confidence that if I confessed my sins, did my penance and took Holy Communion, I was absolved of my sins, and my filthy slate wiped clean by the finger of Almighty God.

Being a good Catholic boy, I prayed a lot in my younger years. One day, I ran out of the house weeping at the thought of losing my parents.

I had this fear of being left all alone in the world. I kept thinking that God was going to take all my loved ones—my parents, my grandparents, even my friends. As I sobbed in my backyard, the sun seemed to get so bright that I was practically blinded.

I heard a voice say: "Son, do not be afraid of death, for it is only the beginning of eternal life with Me. Some of your family will die, but you shall not see death as you know it."

Peace immediately came upon me.

During my young adulthood, as a cop, I was attacked by a biker of a notorious motorcycle gang. He acted like Superman on drugs. Before I could say "freeze, you're under arrest," he pulled out a steel bladed knife.

"You're going to be a dead f____ pig," he snarled.

I took him seriously when he got closer, seeing the crazed fixation in his eyes that he was determined to stab me until I was dead. I had no time to think or even flinch. In seconds my survival instinct kicked in. I drew my revolver from my holster and aimed for his chest, ready to squeeze the trigger to fire a round that would penetrate his heart and stop him dead in his tracks. Suddenly, as I was about to blow the biker away, the woman from hell rose up getting between her man and me, blocking my line of fire.

It all happened so fast, that my pounding heart felt ready to jump out of my chest. I was on full speed ahead. My adrenaline was so high I became like Superman myself.

Quickly, I holstered my gun, grabbed the woman with my other hand, pushing her to the ground. There was no time to retrieve my weapon. I knew it was life or death. It became second nature, save her and disarm the nut.

As the biker lunged at me with his knife, I stepped into him with my knee to his groin. I grabbed his wrist with the knife in hand, turning it away from my body. At the same time my other hand was around his throat squeezing the life out of him. With a death grip I lifted him up off his feet, spun him around towards my patrol car and slammed his body down on the hood. As I watched his body hit that cold metal, his limbs gave way, the knife fell from grip, and he was out cold.

Turning him over face down, I cuffed him and dragged him to the car. Throwing him into the back seat, I began to beat him. I wanted to kill him.

I heard the cry of the woman, "Stop. You're killing him. Please stop." My partner pulled me off him.

As the days went by, I knew I'd lost it. He was out on bail and the biker gang war was on. I was suffering from battle fatigue. I stayed awake for days, drinking more, and using speed to stay alert. I was afraid to go to sleep out of fear that the biker gang would kill me the moment I did.

Finally, I collapsed. I remembered nothing or no one. I experienced amnesia-like symptoms and hallucinated at the same time. While hospitalized, I had a reaction to the medication that was given to me and swallowed my tongue. I stopped breathing, losing consciousness.

I began to fade. I remember leaving my body, turning around and seeing myself lying on the hospital bed. I was drawn towards a brilliant light. It was so bright and yet so clear; I could plainly see three, distinct people.

Before me was the Lord Jesus Christ, ever so wonderful, smiling with open arms. To the left was my maternal grandmother, Anna, who died when I was fourteen. On the right was my uncle Joe, who had also died.

They were all smiling. Then Jesus said, "Go back, my son. It's not your time."

My friend Ron came to visit and found me in this state and ran to the nurses' station for help. God had it all planned out. He used Ron to save my life.

When my parents arrived, my father held me in his arms and cried out to God, "Bring him back to me, I'll do whatever You ask of me Lord, please, just save him!"

God answered. I woke up and told them the awesome experience that happened to me. I was happy to see them, but somehow I felt cheated. I felt better with the Lord.

Strange as it might seem, having to come back was disappointing.

I had another near-death experience one night when I was on the run as a gangster-cop in Little Chicago.

I was strung out on drugs and alcohol again, in fear for my life. This time I enlisted my dad to help me fight the bad guys. The crazy part is that while driving my car with my dad as a passenger, I had a flashback. I was freaked out to the point I didn't even know he was in my car or that it was my dad next to me. I began driving frantically up a one way street, desperately trying to get to my friend's night club. I panicked. Wanting to avoid a head-on collision, I jumped out of the speeding car, leaving my dad behind in the passenger seat. I dove down a one-story deep stairway, then busted through a steel door.

But that didn't get me. I was knocked out cold by a couple of my mob associates who thought I was coming to take them out and kill them.

I fell to the ground, hitting my head on the concrete. From that blow to the head, I lost all body functions. Death came near again.

Once more, my soul left my body and I saw myself on the ground. This time, there was no light waiting for me. Instead, there was only darkness.

Later, I woke up on the floor and there stood my dad. Somehow he stopped my runaway car without a scratch on the car or himself. He parked the car and headed to the club, not knowing what to expect or if I would be alive.

A few members of the mob greeted him and said, "Your son needs your help, Hugo."

As he came to me, I stood up and collapsed into his arms. "Dad, I'm sorry." I said. "I almost killed you, too."

I truly believe I wasn't headed for heaven this time, but God divinely intervened, rescuing me again. Amazingly enough, I felt hurt, but there were no signs of internal or external injuries.

I know today that God's word is true and His plan for me is written in stone. I love the Scripture in Jeremiah 29:11 that says, *"For I know the thoughts that I think toward you, says the Lord, thoughts of peace and not of evil, to give you a future and a hope."*

Mom and Pop and the church tried to teach me good family values when I was a small child. They also tried to impart to me the traditions of the "Italian way."

My mother and grandmother went to several services in Pittsburgh led by Kathryn Kuhlman, a popular evangelist and faith healer. My mother's friends Olga and Mary who sang in Kathryn Kuhlman's choir must have had a revelation from God about me one day because they prompted me to go with them to a service.

I was probably around eight or nine and believed God could do anything. I experienced His presence when He touched me through the prayers of this anointed woman of God.

Who would have ever guessed that years later I would be praying for people the same way? I've discovered that many ex-offenders who were prayed for by Kathryn Kuhlman are also in ministry today. They still talk about having a deeper walk with the Lord.

I loved Mom, Grandma and their friend. I figured they'd had a nice experience. But that's as deep as it went for me.

I was taught I should revere God, the Church, the family and all my elders. But as I tried to do all that, good and evil waged war inside my body. Temptation was everywhere.

When I was twenty-one, my mom convinced the entire family to go to a mass that a priest named Father McDonoughue was celebrating on a weeknight. My mother claimed, "Many people had miraculous healings during his services."

Pop was hobbling around because of his chronic bad knees. No one in the medical profession came up with a cure, so Pop was even willing to spend an extra night in church to see if this Father McDonoughue could help.

Strange things unfolded that night. When the priest prayed for people to be healed, one by one they fell to the floor. I asked what in the world was going on. Someone whispered, "They're being slain in the Spirit." Having no idea what that meant, I stood by, awestruck at how people were reacting to Father McDonoughue's prayers.

Pop's reaction was no different than all the others. As Father McDonoughue laid his hands on Pop's forehead and prayed, I watched my dad's strong, muscular body relax and fall to the floor. One by one, each of the other members of the family went down, like a line of dominos.

I was one of them.

A sense of peace and contentment swept over me as I lay there.

In the days and the first couple of months following this experience, Pop's legs appeared to be free of pain. He no longer needed a cane to help him walk.

Pop's friends scoffed at his claims that he'd been healed by God. They ridiculed any possible healing so often that his so-called "buddies" finally convinced our family that the priest must have pushed so hard on Pop's head that it had caused the domino effect.

Once doubt took over Pop's mind, his pain came back.

Like St. Peter walking on the water, my dad took his eyes off of the Source of his miracle and began believing instead in the screaming wind and towering waves.

Earlier in my life, a young police officer named Tony became my hero. His grandparents, my grandparents and our parents lived in the same neighborhood, Little Chicago.

It was the early 1970s and Tony had come back from serving in Vietnam, after which he'd been recruited into the police force.

He became my idol. I gave serious thought to becoming a police officer myself. Strange as it may be, I was a young wise guy, wannabe cop.

My buddies and I formed what we called "the Seventh Street Gang." Whenever we could during the summer months, we would sleep over at each other's houses so we could sneak out after dark. Our nightly meeting spot was in a rear alley under a dim street light.

A garbage dumpster served as a card table for our poker games. The street light provided just enough light for us to see our cards, but allowed us to slip into the shadows whenever somebody came near.

Tony and the other cool cops would cruise by and check on us, sometimes even joining our games of chance, but mostly to shoot the breeze.

That was police public relations in those days.

It must have worked. New Kensington had the lowest crime rate in the area. The only crime was organized and everybody, including the cops, was aware of it. You seldom heard about someone getting robbed, raped or murdered.

A large percentage of the police force worked with *la famiglia*. Some had a harsh attitude toward justice, which held down serious crime. Suspects with no family connections were often executed the old-fashioned way without benefit of judge or jury.

Troublemakers would disappear so fast that no one ever saw or heard of them again.

We had no crime problem. No disorganized crime problem, that is.

Local crime figures respected our elders, the police, women and children. As a result, anyone could walk safely down the streets after dark. Muggings, assaults, rapes or drug peddling in our streets weren't as prevalent as they are today.

Everything that wasn't controlled by the "boys," the cops shut down. All of us worked together to keep the town safe.

If you wanted a vice, action could be found in our town, but it was kept in the "underground," the underworld of Little Chicago.

In New Kensington, our family ruled by controlling politics at every level of government. We worked within organized labor, too. It was widely accepted, even assumed, that unions had mob connections. Back in those days the working man was heard by the politicians because blue-collar workers were in the majority. Since unions represent votes, they are catered to by the politicians who like being reelected.

Political machines were deep-rooted in every community, controlling the votes and maintaining the power.

Our family used its influence to call the shots, often resorting to force and violence in order to obtain lucrative political positions and keep them. Bribes were a business expense. We stood on the saying, "money talks and people walk."

We had the power to influence anyone, legally or illegally. We also had a way of making an offer that couldn't be refused.

Anyone disputing family decisions could find their health impaired and their future in question.

Getting in the way of family business could send you to the bottom of the Allegheny River wearing cement shoes. Adversaries were dealt with decisively in the days when we were at our peak.

The mob had control of a number of legitimate corporations, which still make up the organization's sphere of influence and control today.

Silk pinstripe suits and wide brim hats are a thing of the past. Today's *famiglia* members dress like anybody else.

The underworld has learned to conform. Its internal structure has provided status for those who would plod along in everyday workclothes as well as those who dress like Wall Street brokers.

Today, organized crime affects all of society, preferring public relations and investments to a punch in the nose or pickpocketing.

The mafia functions as an illegal invisible government whose objective is not competition with the establishment, but nullification of governments' power over them. Mobsters operate lower levels of administration such as bribing a police chief, prosecutor or judge.

That didn't always work. An acquaintance of mine tried to bribe a relative's way out of federal prison, but got snagged by an honest official and ended up serving time himself.

At the upper level are figures that head major agencies and have great political clout. When a family boss supports a candidate for political office, he does so in an effort to gain control and favors. In reality his illegal influence deprives honest citizens of their democratic voice, thus nullifying the democratic process.

The largest single factor in the breakdown of law enforcement is the corruption and connivance of public officials.

As government regulation expands into more and more areas of private business activity, the power to corrupt offers more control over matters affecting the ordinary life of each citizen.

Every crime family has in its division of labor one position for a corrupter. This person bribes, buys, intimidates, threatens, negotiates and sweet-talks himself into a relationship with police, public officials and anyone else who might help family members maintain immunity from arrest, prosecution or imprisonment.

The corrupter is not listed on any organizational chart which informants and police sketch out. And so, the family never uses the term *corrupter,* but only refers to the *corruptee.*

The services provided are varied. Crimes committed by corrupt officials are popular reading in newspaper, radio and TV coverage and are expected to surface sooner or later.

What everyone must realize is that such scandal is put before the public simply to cover up the crimes of others. Corrupters nullify the law enforcement and political process primarily by bribery and other forms of influence such as contributions to political campaigns and promises to deliver votes in a particular area.

Respectable bankers become unwitting allies. Many of the securities stolen in the United States are stored in the vaults of respectable banks and are sometimes used as collateral for legitimate loans.

The mob buys, steals or extorts stolen securities from burglars and robbers. In fact, they often make arrangements for the theft by employing a front man to take the securities to a bank and offer them as the basis for a loan.

Once the transaction has been completed, they only pay the interest through the front man in order to use the clean money for the purpose of corrupting the very governmental and business systems which keep the bankers alive.

The Mafia has a rich history, prospering over the years by their dominant force of rule and reign. Many people think it is fading away.

They're wrong.

Chapter 3

Wine, Women & Song

My mom wished I could have been a saint from birth. I was never the angel she would have liked me to be.

Pop agreed. "You were such a blessing when you were young until you reached fifteen," he said, "then you became something else."

I understand what he meant. Being good was part of my nature until that teenage year when my revolution into manhood began.

Maybe it started with the Beatles who really impressed me. Watching the British imports swagger on TV made a big hit with me as early as age five.

I imagined myself as a big-time musician. I learned to play the guitar. I became obsessed with Tom Jones, imitating him with a shake of my hips. Later, girls at school were captivated. Mom and Pop thought it was cute.

When I reached fifteen, a bunch of my buddies and I teamed up to form a band. We were a hit locally. We became popular in the Pittsburgh area, and I was the leader of the pack.

In my own mind, I was Wayne Newton, Frank Sinatra, Dean Martin, and Jerry Lewis all wrapped up into one ball of marvelous talent, charm and manly sexuality. My good looks, blue eyes, great voice, boyish charm and hot Italian blood all convinced me I was God's gift to women.

"Old Blue Eyes" Sinatra was my number one hero.

Girls flocked around me. My self-importance grew. On weekends our band played in clubs as union musicians. I had my own car and access to the two vans from our family-owned dry-cleaning business. We had no trouble getting our gear from one gig to another.

It gave me an identity and a purpose for living "My Way" as the song goes.

I swaggered. I strutted. I worked on my "look," dressing like a gangster, letting everybody know I was one of *la famiglia's* "*boys*" as I crooned into the microphone. It was quite a combination.

Hamming it up came natural to me. I loved playing the part of being a big shot.

Pop made sure that I had opportunities to earn my own money from the time I was twelve. My band was seen as one more enterprise. It provided me with enough cash to buy my own car, great musical equipment and fancy clothes. It gave me money, local fame, girls and a wardrobe second to none. I already had a family name that carried respect and opened doors.

I enjoyed the stardom.

I projected the image of a playboy-gangster. My dad and grandfather put up with it. They saw it as something else to put up with while a beloved son and grandson found himself.

Pop had me working after school in the parking lots in the city. He was the boss of the Parking Authority. Some evenings I would help run the bingo games at the Sons of Italy club, but whenever I could I was performing in nightclubs and lounges.

One night our band was playing out of town. Usually our parents and friends followed wherever we performed, but this particular evening we were on our own.

As a junior wise guy, I was ready to fight with anybody at anytime. So when a rowdy motorcycle gang pushed its way through the crowd, I stepped up to their challenge.

They weren't real Hell's Angels. They were only "wannabe" bikers. They were motorcycle riders who tried to look and dress the part. They were just local punks.

One of the bikers stood up and threw a quarter at me. The coin bounced off of my treasured Gibson guitar.

Infuriated, I stopped. We'd tolerated their rude, sarcastic manner and foul mouths long enough; it was time to "kick butt." I swaggered over to the biker and dropped the quarter at his feet. "Do you have enough money to pay for a new guitar and your funeral?" I snarled in his face.

The room suddenly grew quiet. I stared him down and told him that the gun in my pocket had the last laugh.

The wannabe bikers decided I was serious enough to do something crazy. They thought twice about starting a brawl. The bikers shuffled out the front door. The club erupted in jeers and catcalls. I was the tough guy and everybody knew it.

I strutted back up to the stage. To the cheers of the crowd, we started playing again.

In the middle of our song, I yelled, "STOP!" and bolted for the door. The band and most of the bar patrons followed. I realized our van was parked out front by the motorcycles.

I'd won the battle inside, but the bikers had gotten the last laugh. As their choppers screamed down the highway, I surveyed the damage to our van. Every tire had been slashed.

Somebody called the cops, but the bikers were long gone.

Another evening, a drunken fan tried to clobber me. He was jealous because I had been flirting with his girlfriend during one of our songs.

A state trooper who was the father of one of the band member's grabbed the guy before he could hit me.

He held me off from going after the guy saying, "Rocco, if you get your hands messed up you can't play the guitar."

I backed away.

The crowd loved it.

I was the *man*.

I was only fifteen, working in lounges, when I bellied up to the bar and ordered my first beer and got served.

The bartenders just assumed I was old enough to be in there, since I was working there.

But I got carried away. I liked the taste. I liked the buzz. I liked the numbing effect of the alcohol. Everything was a laugh. I was a tough guy and everybody liked me.

I graduated from the playground to the barstool. But instead of growing up and getting wiser and better, I retrogressed by becoming addicted to alcohol and nightlife.

Instead of becoming a man, I went backward. I started to think I was a hotshot. I could go into the local bars and get served. They became a hangout for me and my friends of the "Seventh Street Gang."

We were tough guys.

We declared our neighborhood as our own turf, defying any other tough guys to enter. Hanging out there and in pool halls and pizza shops was cool. Actually, we weren't much of a gang.

There were no rumbles, no drug wars. Mostly we just liked to look cool.

Our greatest vice was playing pool. We had poker games at the big table at night after the hall was closed.

Our "big brothers" encouraged us—the pool sharks, professional gamblers, pimps, dope dealers, con artists, thieves and hustlers who knew our fathers. They gave us respect. They were available to teach us lessons you don't learn in school.

One night we were all gathered around the poker table with all the big boys when, suddenly, the wail of sirens filled the air.

Cops banged on our door yelling, "Open up in the name of the law!" Gunfire rang out outside.

Most of the poker players grabbed their money before hitting the floor. Some of us dove for the large pot that had been building up. We grabbed pool sticks to look as though we were in a friendly game of billiards.

The door burst open. Police officers stampeded in, guns drawn. It looked as if we were in for a bust. Adrenaline surged through my body. My heart banged in my chest like a drum in a parade.

Man, I thought, *We're in for it this time.*

The cops stared down their gun barrels at us.

Then, we began to recognize familiar faces. Several of the policemen were family members and close friends, even business associates of our dads, what we called *compe* cops.

One of the officers broke the silence. "Relax. A guy with a gun didn't run in here to hide out, did he?"

Whew! What a relief! Everyone broke out with laughter, including the lawmen. They told us the shot we heard had been fired by a cop. A wounded robber was lying out on the sidewalk. His partner had escaped, and they were hunting him.

Some of the cops spotted our poker game through the window and wanted to have a little fun. Most of them were friends. They decided at the spur of the moment to give us a little scare. They figured it would be a great opportunity to "break our stones." In the name of justice, they broke up our poker game for a minute.

A minute was all we wasted. The cops searched the joint and told us to "carry on," which we did. We even offered to deal them in.

Following their departure, we had to argue about the money, the cards, who had what, and where our seats were.

But we were on our way to adulthood. I know I felt I was a man.

I was ready for the big time, but only one thing was left for me to be completely fulfilled; I was still a virgin.

I plotted for that facet of my life to change. Now that I could hang out in bars, I had plenty of opportunity to be with women.

I had lots of girlfriends, but I never tried much sexually with any of them.

My hot Italian blood burned within me. I wanted to become a real man. I had to know a woman in a carnal way. I couldn't remain a little boy any longer.

I fantasized making love to all the pretty girls I saw. I plotted. I imagined. I daydreamed. I worked myself into a sweat, puzzling my family at the dinner table. Blushing, I could not explain.

I could not tell them I was consumed with fifteen-year-old lust and carnality.

Delirious with my manhood, I vowed to take every woman who dared look at me, let alone any who gave me an inviting smile. I imagined every glance to be a flirting "come and get me if you can."

I rose to the challenge as much as possible.

Women became my favorite pastime. Some girls would let me have my way and some wouldn't. I was determined to find who was who, taking full advantage of those who would and attempting to seduce the ones who wouldn't.

I knew there were women who did it for money. That's where I retreated. I knew I would soon accomplish my goal.

The girls in the "cat houses," the bordellos, the houses of prostitution, were always willing to oblige for a price. Such places were plentiful in those days. Whenever out-of-town "Vegas" type girls were brought in, the patrons lined up like kids in a candy store. When I couldn't get satisfaction from my girl friends, I got it there.

I became addicted to sex as well as with gambling and drinking.

My poor mama. Seemingly overnight, I went from nice little boy to cathouse customer and beer-guzzling lounge lizard. *Big shot.* Nightclub singer.

One of my favorite songs on stage had a line: "Young musician, playboy, wise guy, with all the opportunities to be whoever and whatever you want in life." That was me. I was on a high.

Money and opportunity were no challenge. I lacked nothing of this world! The family had full control of the local nightspots. I was my grandfather's grandson, the young stud, the "Italian Stallion."

I craved the excitement of living life to its fullest and seeing how far I could go. *How far was too far?* Was there a line I couldn't cross?

I exuded such self-confidence that I was certain I could charm a snake. That was the problem. I eventually became one.

I learned all the wrong things fast. I was addicted to gambling which included professional card playing, sports betting, bookmaking, horse handicapping and greyhound racing. Before I knew it, I had my hand in loan sharking, fencing stolen property and confidence games.

I came to know some of the most crooked people in the world. On a scale of one to ten for corruption, Little Chicago definitely deserved a ten plus.

My mom didn't like what she saw, and told me every time an opportunity arose.

Her words had little effect. The mob bosses had it all, and I wasn't going to settle for less. I wanted the whole pie.

Looking at the guys on top, I realized that most of their power and money came from drug connections. No, they didn't go out on the street and do all the peddling. Their sales were never one-on-one. They engineered the biggies. Most dealers didn't even take cocaine, which was the money-maker in those days.

I had no intention of becoming an addict either. Not even a user. Why should I take a drug that would bring in $100 on the streets? Why wouldn't I want to keep the profits for myself? I intended to become the big dealer, but never have any drugs in my possession.

The young heir, the prince of the night, was learning the ropes.

Chapter 4

Cop or Gangster?

Following graduation from high school I enrolled at Duquesne University in Pittsburgh to begin a four-year liberal arts program with the hope of going on to their school of law.

At least that was Pop's dream. He wanted me to become a lawyer. I did not share the dream.

As a little boy I had talked about becoming a doctor. I even wrote out prescriptions on a pad, pretending to be an attending physician. As I grew older, I read medical books to expand my knowledge of medicine. Pop had another dream.

"Rocco, you need to be a lawyer," he told me time and again.

He always talked about the time when I'd be a great attorney. Yet I had ideas of my own.

In my freshman year of college, when Pop ended up under the surgeon's knife to fix his bad knee, I dropped out of college and joined the police force.

I knew he would be furious. I also knew he was going to be laid up for weeks. So, this was my opportunity. Now I could do what I wanted when he couldn't get out of bed to force me to change my mind.

The age requirement to become a cop had been dropped from twenty-one to eighteen, and I took advantage of it.

When Pop came home from the hospital, if he could have gotten out of bed, even with his cast and crutches, I would have been dead, or at least I'd end up back in college with a few broken bones. So, I kept my distance.

Pop had only spanked me a few times when I was young. He didn't usually have to use any force to impact me. He had a certain look that meant, "You'd better listen, Rocco!"

Once when I'd been delving into things Pop didn't approve of he grabbed me by the throat and lifted me to a higher note of understanding.

I gave him a wide berth. It was good he was flat on his back when I announced I was blowing off college.

Classes bored me. My mind was so far away on big business and success, and I only attended sporadically.

When I became a police officer, there were strings attached. The commissioner told me I could only be on the force for two years. Then I would get my butt back in school and become the lawyer that my family wanted me to be. This was the deal he made with my dad and grandfather.

I thought I got in on my own merits, but it was a family connection. I got what I wanted for the moment.

One day while on patrol, I attempted to arrest a hood, Joe Santini (not his real name) in a drug bust. He was under investigation for being a drug dealer. My partner and I observed him doing a drug deal out of his car. We pulled over and got out of our patrol car. We approached his car walking down both sides. As I started opening his door, he suddenly took off. With tires squealing, rocks and dirt flying in our faces, he nearly ran over my feet with his rear tire. I saw "red" and wanted to tear him up. Quickly moving out of the way, I held my steel flashlight firmly in my right hand cocked it behind my back, throwing it with all I had at his rear window. It spiraled right threw the glass, shattering the window and hit him square in the head as he sped down the road.

We ran to our car. My partner called for back up. We sped down the road after him, with sirens blaring, in a high-speed chase, which ended at his house.

He hid out in his mansion which was guarded by steel gates. We had his house surrounded.

"This is the police. Come out with your hands up," yelled the sergeant over the loud speaker of his car.

Within the hour he surrendered, walking out of his house with his hands in the air. He went to jail, and I went to the bar.

The next morning I received a call. "The chief wants to see you in his office now," said the captain. I was still hung over from the night before. I sobered myself up with a cold shower, lots of coffee, and a handful of aspirins so I could face the chief.

What on earth did he want with me, I thought. *Did I screw up? No way. He probably wants to commend me for busting another hood.* Commendation and promotion surely awaited. Was I ever wrong.

As I walked into the chief's office, my mouth dropped wide open. At that moment I knew I screwed up. I arrested a big shots' son who was connected. I was ordered by the chief to drop all charges and apologize. If I apologized to him no charges would be brought against me or the department for police brutality.

I graciously accepted, biting my tongue the whole time. I wanted to tell them all where to go.

I tried to be a good cop, but seeing the sordid side of politics and power, I decided that the judicial system had no hope. Why should I back the law? So I became a gangster cop.

I took drugs from the criminals, and turned around and sold them myself. I did whatever I could to make myself money.

I was out with one of my criminal buddies one night, looking for some action. My friend nurtured a dream of becoming a cop like me, but got busted for drugs. He remained a drug dealer and con artist. He was also a pretty good safe cracker and thief. Nevertheless, he liked acting like a cop, so we were nicknamed Starsky and Hutch, a popular TV cop series at the time. Out looking for action, we drove through town.

As we pulled through an intersection, my buddy, "Hutch," suddenly yelled, "Look out!"

Out of the corner of my eye, I saw an eighteen-wheel semi-truck coming right at us. Just like "Starsky" on the TV show, I spun the car around, avoiding the near-collision.

"Let me at him!" yelled Hutch. In a scream of tire rubber, I took off after that trucker. Hutch reached for the .38-caliber pistol I kept in the glove box.

The trucker was stupid enough to pull over. Before he could even roll down his window, Hutch was up on the rig, flinging the door open and jamming my .38 into the trucker's ear.

The truckers eyes widened in fear.

Hutch went through his manifest and found nothing in the trailer worth hijacking. So he took the trucker's wallet and told him we were even.

But it didn't end there. The trucker went to the cops and told them what had happened. It didn't take the sergeant on duty too long to figure out who had done it. They calmed the trucker down and sent for us.

Two *compe* cops came to the joint where we were hanging out and told us we had to come to the station because the trucker wanted to press charges. I knew I could be in a lot of trouble if I didn't persuade the man to forget he even came to our town. I went in, calm and cool. The sergeant played it up, chewing me up and down, and told me to apologize to the trucker.

I agreed. Two hours later, I came out smiling as a victor. What nobody knew was I almost had to beg him to forget the whole thing. My nice-guy routine worked. A little money for his inconvenience didn't hurt either.

"My partner is psychotic, a mental patient with papers to prove it." I told him. "It would be in your best interest to drop the whole thing because he would not think twice about blowing your head off."

"You have nothing to worry about as long as you leave and never come back to our community. If you drop the charges, my friend will forget the incident after he wakes up tomorrow and all will be well."

The trucker promised to never come back and made me promise to keep "Psycho" away from him.

Another time, Hutch called from the Galaxy nightclub, "Get over here, the boys are in trouble."

Hutch and some of the other wise guys ran a club in the heart of the action.

I got there quickly and went to the backroom where a serious meeting was taking place. The executive board was in session.

My *compes* were in the drug business and had just been taken down by a biker gang. The bikers had bought a large shipment of drugs from them with counterfeit money. This was a major problem since the drugs actually belonged to the mob, and they were expecting to be paid in real cash.

We put together a battle plan and put it into action. Knowing what we did about the bikers, we started with the second-in-command, telling him that he had twenty-four hours to get the cash or he would die, along with any of his dirtbag friends who wanted to become heroes.

We shook down every bar where the bikers hung out and staked out the club president's house, waiting for him to return. Our plan was to kidnap him and trade him for the money. Apparently word got out that we were looking for him, so he didn't come home.

Not long afterward, we were back at the nightclub plotting our next move when in came the biker president with his enforcers. He was as enormous as the comic book character

"The Hulk," and his friends were bigger. He grabbed our doorman by the throat and was about to snap his neck. The doorman couldn't reach for his gun, so from all the way across the club, I jumped up on the bar yelling "Police!" with my gun drawn and leveled at his head. "Freeze, you scumbag," I ordered.

The music stopped. Dancers, bartenders, patrons, waitresses, musicians and the tough-guy enforcers all hit the floor.

The biker dropped our doorman and ran for his Cadillac, his guns blazing. Hutch beat me out the door and was already shooting at him when I dashed outside and felt a bullet go through my hair. That made me so mad that I emptied my gun on them. I shot up their car, hit houses and street lights, but could not hit them. We shot up everything but the bad guys. This was weird, since I was a straight shot and never missed on the target range.

That night, I believe, God intervened.

The bartender had hit the silent alarm. Soon, cop cars screamed from every direction surrounding the club. Some took off after the Cadillac, which was hightailing it out of town.

The police officers took our guns and, once again, I was at the station, explaining this time to the lieutenant.

The cops arrested the bikers and chastised me for actions unbecoming of a police officer. I told them I had been drinking when those unruly thugs entered the bar and began accosting the doorman and threatening the public.

The lieutenant didn't buy it, and got my dad and other family members out of bed to get to the bottom of it.

After one of the bosses came over and talked to the cops, we were released and told there would be no charges against us or the bikers. They knew the mob would take care of this personally.

I had to meet with the under-boss of the entire family. I told him that we attempted to retrieve the money.

On the strength of my word, the boss ordered mob soldiers to get the biker on the telephone and make him an offer he couldn't refuse.

He refused anyway.

That began a saga that is still history in the annals of the American Mafia. Before that war was over, the Feds had infiltrated Little Chicago, pulling off the biggest sting operation in the history of New Kensington.

The biker president was a suspect in a murder. He was arrested by the local authorities and then sprung by the Feds after he agreed to be a snitch.

The Feds targeted us. They already recruited a wise guy informant who was telling them everything he knew about us. He and the biker helped them set up a sting that netted the Feds one of their biggest cases in western Pennsylvania ever. It collapsed an entire drug empire.

Why were the Feds interested in our operation? What started the whole thing was an armored-car heist that took place in downtown New Kensington. The Feds were furious because millions of dollars was stolen in broad daylight and nobody saw or knew anything.

They declared war on the mob. One of their targets disappeared. Another was apprehended, tried, convicted and sent to prison. The mastermind of the heist died of old age without a single charge being filed against him.

Whatever happened to the armored-car loot? By the time everybody took their cut, it wasn't worth the price that the New Kensington family had to pay.

During the course of this fiasco, many wise guys were arrested and sent to prison. A lot of the bikers were sent away too. Even the snitch eventually messed up and was imprisoned. The irony is that none of this would have happened had the big boss of our family taken me up on my offer to take out the biker president for them.

I knew from my other sources that he had become a snitch. The mob decision-makers chose to let him live, because they believed his promise to pay them back, but he never did.

After I was nearly killed the previous year by a biker in the line of duty and ended up in the hospital from "Battle Fatigue," the biker was released on a technicality. Hatred against the biker and against the law that had let my assailant go ate at me.

My belligerent attitude did nothing to make me a worthwhile police officer. My superiors warned me about the chip on my shoulder. Their warnings didn't change my actions or feelings, and they finally laid me off to collect unemployment and a lump sum pension, which wasn't much. In reality I was politely "fired."

Outraged, I vowed a vendetta against all the politicians who were part of the "machine" that ran the politics and decided the fate of many like me. I was out to get even.

For a few years I ran the streets with madness in my heart. Rages of anger warred within me. I possessed the mind of a small-time warlord, devising schemes and games of vengeance.

I feared no one—not the cops, other wise guys, no one. Yet I carried three guns. What would you call that?

I associated closely with *la famiglia* and became a part of the young crew determined to take over and run the town. However, the old crew had no intention of lying down and dying for me and my know-it-all *compes*. They didn't agree with us and tried to discourage the members of our new gang from being part of our circle.

Why were they acting as they did? I didn't understand then. The older group was wiser. They wanted us to become something better and not get involved with the mob or its curse of evil. Looking back, I know they were right even though they were wrong themselves.

They felt as if they had no other choice and they believed we did. If we would just use our intellect, we could legally accomplish things.

I stood my ground and kept on doing everything my way. Never taking the time to reason with anyone, I reacted before I ever stopped to think. Like a firecracker, I'd blast off without warning. My wise guy days were filled with terror and excitement. Adrenaline flowed through my veins as I went through several years of what I considered to be big-time fun.

At night I entertained friends, reveling in wine, women and song, dancing and gambling into the wee morning hours, playing poker, drinking, carousing, betting, overseeing collections and protecting the interests of the select few who controlled Little Chicago. I got involved in the drug trafficking that became the big money-maker, associating with some of the biggest drug dealers in the country.

Some are dead. Others are in prison. Many are still in action. A few are completely reformed and following the straight and narrow. They are rare.

During those days I ran a game on everyone. I tested the law as a cop, and then crossed the line to become a gangster. I was always looking for a hustle, a get-rich-quick scheme—whatever it took to make a buck so I wouldn't have to work hard like my dad.

I wanted everything, and I wanted it now.

I wasn't about to wait for it. As a matter of fact, I was overly anxious, yearning to be successful. My only problem was that I didn't want to work for it. I thought I was too smart for all that and that everything should come easy, handed to me on a silver platter. I was foolish at heart, playing kids' games in an adult world.

During all the craziness I even tried my hand at acting. I was cast as an extra in the movie, *Knightriders*, by George Romero. I was in the big league now. I had only one setback—

myself. Showing up late and strung out, the casting director and even George wanted to cast me in a different role and were willing to cast me in other movies. Real opportunity was knocking at my door. But the day of the final shoot was the day we got into the mob war with the motorcycle gang over the drug deal gone bad. I was stuck on stupid, choosing my gangster life and mafia friends over my new acting career, which turned into a lifetime of regret.

I had learned karate from a friend who was one of the best. I was good with weapons; he was good with his hands and feet. I needed that cutting edge.

I also enjoyed testing the tolerance of the mob and irritating some of the most powerful businessmen and politicians in our area. Most of all, I tested the endurance of my own family. My grandfather Rocco was a very caring and patient man who never turned his back on me.

He and Pop saved me from many "close encounters" with irked underworld figures who wanted to take me out. Only because of who they were did I live.

One of the best hustlers of our time stated, "A master of deceit and deception took down the mob for a few shekels." He was talking about me. Me!

I schemed against the "boys," my own family, friends and foe alike and conned the bookies just for fun.

Looking back now, I realize how foolish my actions were. I tried more than once, but never could succeed in murdering anyone in cold blood.

I pounded mercilessly on people and shot rounds of ammunition at criminals, but never killed anyone, even though I was a skilled sharpshooter.

As a cop, I was determined to kill the biker who came after me and nearly killed me. However, I couldn't do it.

Another guy got me so infuriated I shot at least twelve rounds at him and another dozen rounds at his car as he sped into the night. Yet, despite my skill on the firing range, I never hit him once.

Others got blackjacked; many heads, faces and bones got broken, but no one ever died.

I continued to perform with nightclub bands. All through my teens and twenties, I maintained a daytime good guy image, and then turned into a playboy gangster at night.

Because of who I was, I had it all. *La famiglia* controlled everything, so me and mine lacked nothing. I had my heart's desire in wine, women and song every night. Who can resist the temptation when you're given *carte blanche?*

Big nightclubs and notoriety were mine. Yet I wanted more.

My desire was to be the boss who ran the city. I wanted to be a Don that everyone feared and respected.

My friends and I did not lack nerve. Groomed by wise guys who seemingly had the wisdom of Solomon, whom I thought had the IQs of Einstein, and at least in my opinion had the courage of King David, no Goliath stood in our way.

We believed we could conquer an enemy of any size. The irony is that we believed we were the chosen ones to carry on a great legacy.

We rationalized our own foolish lies. We believed we were above the law. I now admit to having played the role of a fool, but I would have dared anyone to have called me that then.

I was so out of control that my own dad said, "I have never seen such craziness. If you don't kill yourself someone is going to kill you!" He told my mother he wanted to shave my head to see if "666" was tattooed on it.

Heavy on alcohol and drugs, running wild, thinking the party would never end, I was struck with the news that my grandmother was rushed to the hospital.

As I ran into the emergency room I saw my grandfather over her yelling, "Oh Maria, why did you leave us!"

I was too late. She was gone.

I fell apart, just like my grandfather. For the next six months I tried to drown my sorrows in more alcohol and more drugs, trying to kill the pain. I fell into a deep depression to the point I considered suicide. As much as I wanted to blow out my brains, I didn't have the guts.

One late night as my friend drove me around town, drunk as a skunk and high as a kite, I decided to relieve my anger. Rolling down the passenger side window and retrieving my pistol from my shoulder holster, I began firing aimlessly at storefront windows. No one was out on the streets, but soon the sound of burglar alarms reared out as the glass windows shattered from the penetration of my bullets.

I thought nothing of it as we sped away in the heat of the night. Acting psychotic was natural for me. I was filled with so much anger; there was no telling who would be on the receiving end of my wrath in those days of terror.

Chapter 5

Love and Marriage

For years Mom had fussed and fumed over my continuous chain of girlfriends. Some of the girls I brought home for my parents to meet. There were others I hoped they'd never even hear about. My mother was certain I'd never find one girl with whom I would settle down and get married.

I was dating a stunning, knockout blonde when I met another girl who started out as just a good friend. The friendship bloomed and soon we were serious about each other. On Christmas Eve I dumped the blonde and made a commitment to my new love.

I wanted to be with this young lady all the time.

We talked about having a family and then I found myself standing at the altar, pledging to love and cherish her until "death do us part."

Our first months of married life were pure bliss. Soon we were expecting a baby. No doubt about it, we would have a boy, and I'd name him "Rocco Morelli the third."

When my wife gave birth, I was the father of a beautiful baby girl. Her mother said she wanted to give our daughter a name as close as possible to mine. So our darling baby girl became "Racquel."

I was truly happy for the first time in years. Somehow our new little family gave me a sense of contentment that I'd never experienced before. Nothing would ever go wrong again, or so I thought.

I ran for public office, Pennsylvania State Constable in the Fifth Ward. I called on my two best friends to join in the race. We ran as a trio in each of our respective districts.

I won.

Overcome with joy and jubilation I told my wife, "This is only the beginning. We are going on to bigger and better things."

Already licensed as a private detective, I took on two other partners to do security and investigative work. After opening a notary public and tax office, I enjoyed the limelight of being a well-known businessman, husband, father, politician and even a humanitarian.

I led fund-raising drives for well-doing in the community. Feeling high and mighty, I made allegiances with powerful politicians and family underworld figures.

Through my family and friends, I made deals for the future. I was to take a government position in the state and pursue even higher levels of public office. My goal was to get even with anyone who had persecuted me or had not supported my political career. I was going to even things up with anybody who had not helped me gain power, fame and fortune.

Vengeance was mine. I manipulated the system to obtain favors, using fear and intimidation to get what I wanted. I conned people into liking me and was always able to win my constituents with my charm and charisma.

The thing I forgot was the fact that while I built up my own fan club, I also created a long list of enemies. For example, the opposition looked down on me as Public Enemy Number One. Their people were outraged that the heir apparent of the local underworld held public office. They talked with their law enforcement friends. Focus was placed on me and my activities. Bullheaded, I ignored such threats, I feared no one.

It was as if I had a death wish.

Chapter 6

Targeted

My bosom buddy, the best friend I had all through my childhood, tried to persuade me to get involved in his drug business. Drug cartels impacted the world of organized crime. They infiltrated our cities with their junk. The love of money tempted me into their world. My lust for action made me want more.

The Feds were cracking down on mobsters. New Kensington became a target. Headlines indicated they were making progress. Each day another member of *la famiglia* was arrested. One by one people I knew got busted. I vowed that wasn't going to happen to me.

In Little Chicago, everyone that had something to do with the mob had a nickname—Big Rock, Little Rock, Fighting Tony, The Greek, The Candyman, Sam the Man, Joe Buck, Fast Buck, Jo Jo, Big Pete, Little Pete, Boss-Man, Smokey Joe, Joe Bananas, Toto, Dock, The Frog, Big Joe, Little Joe—and too many others to mention.

These were code names that opened closed doors in places where most people dared not go. These were code names that the Feds eventually connected to real names as they focused in on us and our activities.

Many of those people are dead. Some still make their moves. A few have changed, even gone straight. But I remember them all.

I also recall the cons we pulled. I remember every vice, every game I ever ran, every scheme and con that I cooked up with my friends and mentors. Some of those guys were heroes of the old days—men of honor and respect, masterminds who had manipulated their big-money business schemes into vast financial empires.

Multilevel marketing scams were nothing new. A marketing con by the name of Charles Ponzi created the pyramid scheme which became known as the "Ponzi Scheme." This was a racketeering scam that took investors on a promise of great return on their investment. Only a few at the top got rich, like Ponzi, and the rest earned next to nothing. We had ours too; loan sharking, chain letters, lotteries, scratch tickets, bingo games and sports betting to name a few. We took sports bets on any event, from horse, dog, and car racing, to high school, college, and pro games. We were in the midst of the action and had our own version of Las Vegas in Little Chicago.

Whatever commodity was hot as the time, we had it at a price that couldn't be beat—designer clothes, suits, leather and fur coats, diamonds and gold jewelry. Remember the Cabbage Patch dolls in the 1980s? We had them by the truckloads. We had your heart's desire. If we didn't, we could get it with no problem.

In addition to these schemes, drugs, women, gambling and every vice known to man were available in Little Chicago, 24/7.

Caesar was Italian, and his curse remained. There were many little Caesars in places such as Little Chicago. Theirs is the power and riches of days gone by. In the underworld there is big money in providing illicit activities and pleasure for the rest of the world. Gambling, loan-sharking, laundering money, prostitution and the big money business of drugs are supply and demand commodities.

We knew bankers, judges, politicians, doctors, movie stars, professional sports players, cops, gangsters and common folks from all walks of life looking for action. Many who supposedly guard our way of life are accessible for a price. Money talks, as do favors, payoffs, power, lust of all sorts, and just the thrill of life in the fast lane. Everyone wants to be on track for the big score. Rich and famous, living on the edge, whatever makes the adrenaline flow, someone, somewhere, is always looking for the action, which can be obtained for a price.

The mob ran Little Chicago. Mayors, police, state, county, and local officials answered to a boss who answered ultimately to the boss of all bosses. But there were many who wanted to be under bosses.

One Mayor's race became an all-out boxing match. It was like a rival Mafia war over the politics of who was going to run the town in the future.

The opposing candidate, a friend of mine, was well liked by half of the mob, but the other half wanted the incumbent Mayor reelected to office. Families were split over it and people got hurt. Police and Fire Departments were divided. Practically every one in the city took a side for their candidate.

Election Day arrived, and everybody came out to vote. People were escorted to the polls by mob wise guys. Even $50 and $100 bills floated around to persuade the undecided vote for the incumbent Mayor to win. My friend, the underdog, lost by a good margin.

What my friend and his team didn't realize was that the old Mafia regime couldn't take a chance on shifting the power to a newcomer. It wasn't personal; it was just business as usual in Little Chicago.

As racketeers we were ready, willing and able. Our customers encompassed all life-styles, from the working man to the elite. There were rich junkies and poor ones.

Our political friends came from all levels of government. It was all about money, power and self-gratification. Some wanted sex, others drugs and many gambled. We took care of them, and they took care of us. We knew their deep, dark secrets—from prostitutes entertaining high rollers, celebrities, and politicians to getting their fix on coke; from betting big time money on sports games to losing thousands at the underground casinos.

In the end we owned them for life. At any time we could call in a marker. Sports pros were called upon to throw games and shave points to cover the spread that bookies needed to beat the odds. Whether it was government contracts awarded to our friends in exchange for kickbacks and votes, or favor in a criminal investigation, we had the power to make it happen. There were murder trials that were influenced to find defendants not guilty, convictions overturned, charges dropped, and cover-ups all the time.

Whether it was gambling, drugs, sex or simply the desire to have power, it was a compelling, evil force that drove you to no limits. Once hooked, it consumed you and controlled you.

I was a buffer, a go-between, connecting mobsters to those of influence. It was all about favors. If we did you a favor you owed us one in return. We would collect on it at some point and you better have answered the call.

I was called upon to negotiate deals and collect on debts. My good looks, charisma and brains did not outweigh my quick hot-blooded Italian temper. I was the Sonny character in the movie *The Godfather*, charming but deadly. If we met in public you were pretty safe; if you were to take a ride with me, or meet me somewhere, you were in trouble.

I could put a gun to anyone's head and they would agree to anything I demanded. Do it or die. That was their choice.

One politician who tried to do things his way was taken for a ride and made the classic offer he couldn't refuse. He accepted and was handsomely rewarded for life. It was usually a lifetime proposition, which was a lot better than disappearing.

My wise guy mentality knew no bounds. I rode along with the best of cops and gangsters. I experienced the greatest of worldly pleasures and felt the worst pains, both emotionally and physically. I remember the bloody fights and gun battles, the broken bones, the busted heads, the people who lived and those who died.

In the 1980s the Feds cracked down on us, because someone masterminded a scheme that took down an armored car loaded with cash in front of a busy bank one afternoon. Ironically enough, no one saw who did it. It turned out to be an inside job. One guy took the fall while another got whacked and disappeared like Jimmy Hoffa.

During that time, a notorious motor cycle gang tried to move in on our drug market. Their barbarian tough guy act didn't impress us a bit. Instead, blood was spilled on the streets of Little Chicago, and it wasn't ours. Funny thing, the president of the club was arrested for murder, but his charges were dismissed. The FBI flipped him into a confidential informant, with a ticket to buy and sell drugs. He used counterfeit money to buy them from the mob. It didn't take long, until this arrangement went sour on him and the Feds. He was one of the lucky ones who lived to talk about it; he was later convicted and sentenced to prison.

There was one thing I never did. I was not about to be caught with drugs in my possession or be accused of being a pusher.

I didn't dirty my hands by handling such stuff in person. I knew better than that. Plus, now I was an elected public figure.

But I made a serious error in judgment: I trusted a partner in crime.

When you've grown up with a buddy who is as close as a brother, you don't contest his requests or decisions, especially since he's never questioned your wild schemes.

My wife, baby daughter and I were living in a plush upstairs apartment over my grandfather's cleaning establishment. One day, my *compe* friend came to me with a plea for help.

The more I heard of it, the more I wanted none of it. Yet how could I turn him down?

"Rocco," he said, "I need you to keep this stuff for me tonight. I will pick it up tomorrow."

I stared at what he wanted me to keep for him— a small stash of cocaine.

"Look, Tony," I said, "I'd do anything for you, but you know how I feel about handling coke. I just don't want any part of it."

I had a bad feeling in my gut. Something didn't seem right. I was taught to trust your instincts, to go by your gut feeling and never do it if you have second thoughts. The whole thing smelled like trouble. Could this be a trap?

Naah, I thought, not my buddy Tony. He couldn't be a rat. I've known him since I was a kid. He's my friend and a stand-up guy. He would never do such a thing to me.

Tony persisted. "Ah, come on, Rock, what can happen? I'll get it in the morning." After much pleading on his part, I finally gave in.

Taking it upstairs with me, I put it in what I felt would be a safe place.

The next day while my wife and daughter were out shopping, the doorbell rang downstairs. I went down the steps with a gun hidden under my robe.

We had a closed iron gate protecting us from intruders, but when I saw Tony there, I willingly unlocked it.

I was glad to see him. A sense of relief flooded through me. No doubt he had returned to retrieve his property.

"I've come for the stuff," he whispered to me as I opened the gate to admit him and his companion.

I told Tony and the stranger, "Stay outside while I go get your stuff. I don't want you to mess up my carpet with your dirty, wet shoes." It was wintertime and this was my excuse to keep them out of the house.

As I went upstairs to get the coke, my gut was churning. Something was not right. The guy with him looked familiar. "Where have I seen him before?" I asked myself.

"Here's your coke. Now get out of here." I quickly told Tony. Tony handed the coke to the stranger and the stranger handed him a wad of money, which Tony handed to me.

"What's this for? It's your stuff, keep the money." I said.

We started arguing back and forth, and his friend was getting nervous. "Come on Tony," said the stranger, "Let's go." Tony turned away with me holding the loot.

Before I knew it, the stranger flashed a badge and pointed a gun at me.

I slammed the door, but couldn't get it locked. My Italian temper began to flare. How I would have liked to have flattened him, the *snitch!* But I could hear other cops coming.

I said to myself, "If they see this gun on me I'm dead!"

I ran up the steps. I was going to hide the gun and flush the money down the toilet. I only got as far as hiding the gun.

The swat team stormed my home, and I knew I had to surrender. They would have liked nothing more than to see Rocco Morelli dead.

They threw me to the floor, putting their cold revolvers to the back of my neck, and handcuffed me.

My wife and daughter arrived home as I was being taken away.

"What the hell are you doing with dirty wet shoes on?" She screamed. "Why are you taking my husband? Where are they taking you?"

My baby girl started crying. As I was escorted out I told my wife, "Call my dad and don't worry. I will be back home tonight."

I'd been betrayed by one of my closest friends! He'd been caught in a sting and they offered him a reduced prison time if he would help them hook a big fish—me, the elected public servant, heir to a local Mafia family.

The whole thing was a total setup. I was arrested for possession of a fraction of an ounce of cocaine that belonged to my *compe.*

On the way to jail in the squad car, I had time to consider the predicament I was in. No one would ever believe that I was simply doing a pal a favor.

Some pal, I thought as I contemplated what was ahead of me. I had been guilty of a lot of shady deals during my years as a wise guy, but this was ridiculous.

It seemed unreal that I would be doing time for a crime that I hadn't even engineered or committed. Yet there was no doubt about what had taken place. I was caught with drugs in my possession.

The undercover cop thought I recognized him and that he was a dead man. That explains why he froze when I first saw him. I should have listened to my sixth sense.

My career as a public servant was finished. My picture hit the newswires, and relatives across the country called as they heard the news that I had been busted for possession, conspiracy and distribution of drugs.

The media labeled me the "Wall Street Gangster."

The FBI swept through Little Chicago and arrested guys who I had known, who'd been part of the family's backbone for a long time.

Chapter 7

My Alibi

As I prepared for trial, I was torn. I suffered wild mood swings. First I would be euphoric with confidence. Then I would be in the pits of despair. At times, I thought I would be able to beat all the charges against me. My family hired the best lawyers and an investigative team that sought to destroy the prosecution's case.

Other times I trembled in fear. I didn't want to go to prison.

I considered having my former pal knocked off. I pondered blowing him away myself.

The authorities tried to play mind games with me, offering me deals that would have freed me from prison, but would force me to testify against everyone I had ever known.

They wanted my dad and my grandfather. I refused.

In the darkness of my own doubts, I searched for answers. I tried to figure where I went wrong. I even thought about God.

I had friends turn religious and come "witness" to me. They talked about Almighty God as if He was their best friend. They invited me to share that relationship with my Creator. I thanked them, but put it off to another day.

Now, I thought about God. I tried to remember what I had been told about His Son. I heard about Him from my longtime buddy Frank Iozzi, a local doctor, who always put me back together after the scraps.

"You know, Rocco, you need to know Jesus," he volunteered a number of times.

I always put him off.

But Doc Iozzi had no game. He kept bringing it up out of some great compassion and kindness that was totally incomprehensible to me.

I'd seldom seen such love and caring in any other people. Was it his profession of his faith in Jesus Christ that made the difference? My mother also harped about everyone needing to "know Jesus."

She hammered me on it for so long that I simply pushed the phrase aside. What could they possibly mean?

I was a former altar boy. I went to confession. Well, I hadn't gone in a while, but I could have gone if I felt like it. I was still in good standings at church. My priest would have welcomed me and would have heard my confession. After all, since babyhood I'd gone to church every Sunday, and I even had that supernatural experience at the mass with Father McDonoughue.

For me, that night with Father McDonoughue remained memorable. I was just a young man. It had made a deep impression. I hadn't gone completely into my rebellious period, not yet.

It was my first taste of someone claiming, "You need to know Jesus in a personal way." I didn't know what that meant then, nor did I understand it later when Doc Iozzi began talking much the same way.

Awaiting trial, I was released on bail. Although I was still free and could go wherever I pleased, somehow I already felt imprisoned. Hate became a prison of its own.

I plotted my revenge against my betrayer. I felt such bitterness and hatred toward my former best friend that it consumed me. The mob knew my strengths and weaknesses. Tony was to be silenced once and for all. I was the one to do the hit. The "Boss" proposed me for membership, a Made Man, what I always wanted. The only catch: "Whack Tony."

While in Doc Iozzi's office one day, he handed me these tickets, "I have six tickets to the Full Gospel Business Men's dinner on Friday night. Why don't you get some friends and go? The tickets are on me."

I stared at him. He didn't add, "It might do you a world of good," but I knew what he was thinking.

"Thanks," I answered. "I don't know who I'll get to go with me, but I'll be there."

I hardly spoke the words before I began to regret them. I wanted to give myself a swift kick. Why had I been so stupid as to accept his invitation to go to something as far-out as a— what? A *Full Gospel Business Men's* dinner? A Business Dinner Gospel Show?

The people I chose to accompany me that night had to be the strangest assortment ever to show up at a Full Gospel Business Men's Fellowship dinner, but the most amazing invited guest of all was my former best friend, Tony.

When I told my *compes* we were going to dinner, I wasn't being evangelistic. No, I was following Pop's lifelong advice to "keep your enemies closer than a brother."

Pop always told me to keep your enemies close to you and keep tabs on what they are doing. I also needed the perfect alibi. This would be the night, the night I would whack Tony. How sweet it is I thought. "What better alibi than having a bunch of church folk vouch for me."

I figured out a plan that would allow me to get away with the perfect crime. No one would ever suspect I had anything to do with Tony's disappearance. It would be another Hoffa story. "Whatever happened to Tony?"

When my strange entourage and I walked into the meeting, we found it filled with happy, smiling people toting Bibles and handing out little magazines full of Christian testimonies.

My *compes* and I fumbled with our little magazines and took our places at a table. Before we could eat, however, we all stood as they sang and prayed.

Before we arrived that night, I decided I would act just like them. Whatever they would do, I would do. But never in my life had I witnessed such a scene, and I'd been to a lot of fancy places. Faces radiated as the assembly worshipped with their hands raised in the air.

I gripped mine tightly behind me. With all the mental pressure I'd been under since the arrest, the atmosphere of the evening was strangely refreshing. The joy that these people seemed to be experiencing caught my total attention. Were they just a bunch of kooks, or were they as happy as they appeared to be?

Glancing at my companions I saw a nervous gang who looked out of sorts.

What next?

Nobody lit up a cigar. Nobody started yelling catcalls, like "Hey, man, where are the dancing girls?"

My friends were perplexed, but respectful. It was as if they were also trying to measure the sincerity of these men and women shouting, "Praise the Lord!" and "Hallelujah!"

My discomfort grew. I felt an urgency to get out of there quickly and as far as possible from these religious nuts. I debated whether to slip out, pretending to look for the rest room, or if I should just stand and excuse myself politely.

No matter how badly I wanted to get away, I couldn't move. I stood there, spellbound. One by one, my *compes* made discreet exits, going back and forth to the bar outside the meeting room. Why wasn't I fleeing too?

Following the speaker's introduction, I felt compelled to listen. After all, Frank had given me the tickets.

The master of ceremonies said the guest speaker's name was Steve Totin, and his job was Ministry Director at Cornerstone Television in Wall, Pennsylvania.

A tall, thin man with graying hair and glasses stood and walked to the podium. He looked like any guy you might have met on the street, but as he began to tell his story, his message held my attention.

Steve had been a hard core teamster that who worked for the Labor Unions and had been consumed by hate.

Steve told about leaving his wedding anniversary party early one morning with an inebriated relative because they'd run out of beer. The guy drove like an idiot and wound up going over a barrier into a parking lot, not only damaging the car, but also doing extensive damage to Steve's head.

As his life story unfolded, the speaker had me drawn in as if I, too, was experiencing his pain and frustration.

In the months following his accident, he fought an uphill battle to recovery. He realized that he needed to find a good lawyer as his bills piled up and his financial woes grew. He sought the advice of an attorney who said he needed money up front in order to represent him.

Steve scraped the money together to pay the smooth talking attorney, but nothing happened.

Time passed, and still nothing happened. The lawyer quit returning his phone calls.

The attorney did very little on Steve's behalf. His promises never materialized. Steve's frustration as well as his bills kept mounting.

Disgust and anger grew into intense hate. The attorney had promised he'd win thousands of dollars for his pain and suffering. Instead, he just charged Steve hundreds of dollars an hour. Steve's financial problems grew, but the lawyer took nearly all the money that he could pull together.

"I literally wanted to kill the guy," recalled Steve.

Sitting there listening to his testimony, I couldn't help but compare our lives. I'd been so embittered by my former friend's betrayal.

I'd wanted to rub him out. Fit him with cement shoes, and feed him to the fishes.

Did I really think I would get away with whacking Tony without making myself the obvious culprit? Nobody had both the motive and the means more than I.

Did I want to face a murder rap on top of all my other legal woes? The judge deciding my sentence would put me away for life.

Steve continued to share his testimony. He told how his wife Dorothy had started a prayer meeting in their home once a week.

With all their financial and physical woes, he said, he didn't need a wife who'd gone off the deep end spiritually. He scoffed at the idea of prayer doing anything of value, so when her friends gathered to pray, he retreated to a neighborhood bar. There he sat in anger, resenting their intrusion on *his* home and *his* life.

He went on about how his wife became determined to go to a local church where Russ and Norma Bixler, who later founded Cornerstone Television, were ministering at a weekly prayer meeting. When Dorothy came out from those services each week, she was bubbling over with excitement over all the healings, signs and miracles. Steve would scoff, choosing instead to wait outside by the car. One evening, Steve's curiosity got the best of him, and he decided to wander inside and see what was taking place.

While sitting in one of the back pews, he was amazed to find himself responding to the altar call. To Steve's amazement he found himself praying for somebody else to be healed. Even more astounding was that the person claimed his symptoms were gone!

This episode turned out to be the beginning of Steve's coming to know Jesus personally. From that night on, he began to search the Bible for answers and to seek a deeper walk with the Lord.

Steve also experienced a physical miracle, a healing from all the physical problems he'd suffered since the accident. He said he also experienced a "circumcision of the heart," and that it resulted in him feeling the wall of hatred and anger he'd built up against his attorney crumble.

After he accepted the Lord, Steve said, he no longer had that same urge for vengeance.

Yet, Steve declared, after meeting Jesus, he did not find total peace. That did not come until he confronted the lawyer in person, shared what had taken place and forgave the man. The greedy lawyer had an attack on his own conscience and offered to make some financial restitution to Steve.

As he finished, I felt a strange stirring inside me. It was like nothing I'd never experienced before.

Steve declared that without Jesus residing in his heart, he would never have been able to forgive all those who had wronged him. Without Jesus, he would never have been able to let all the bitterness toward the lawyer be erased as if it had never existed.

I knew right then and there that I was no different. The seething hatred that had driven me for so long had to go. If it did not, I'd never find peace.

Steve said "It takes a real man to stand for Jesus. The shortest verse in the bible says 'Jesus wept.' Are there any real men here tonight that want to experience His love and forgiveness and *peace?*"

I rushed from my seat.

I wanted that peace.

It was as if a magnet was drawing me, as if someone threw me out of my seat. If ever anybody yearned for peace, it was *me*.

I thought of my mom and all the prayers that she had said for me.

My mother had anguished over my ungodly life-style. How she'd wept over the wrongs I'd done. Was the Lord finally going to honor her fervent pleas? Was my godly mother responsible for my winding up in this place? I had no way of knowing for sure, but one thing I was certain; I had to meet Jesus personally.

I knew a prison term still awaited me, but being in a physical jail didn't concern me nearly as much as remaining in the tormenting, vengeance-filled prison of my mind.

I no longer wished to be driven by a desire to retaliate against anyone who'd ever done me wrong.

Steve said Jesus freed him from all the things that had eaten him up in the past.

That was what I needed.

"Oh, Jesus," I pleaded, "help me let go of the sins and let You come into my heart. Please, please, Lord, help me find peace."

Steve asked me what it was that I needed prayer for.

"Can this Jesus do for me what He has done for you? I'm about to go to prison, and I can't even tell you what I was going to do tonight."

There, before hundreds of total strangers, I bowed my head as Steve prayed for me.

I fell to the floor.

For the second time in my life, I became oblivious to everyone and everything around me.

I felt as if Jesus was there beside me, forgiving my past and loving me. I have no idea how long I laid there, basking in His presence, but I do know I had no desire to move. Tears that hadn't flowed in years flowed freely down my cheeks. All those years bottled up inside.

They were not tears of sorrow, only joy.

My whole countenance changed. The darkness left. There was a glowing about me.

When I returned to my feet, Steve's wife, Dorothy, came over.

"The Lord told me I needed to pray for you to receive the Baptism of the Holy Spirit," she said.

She prayed, placing her hands on my forehead. Power, almost like electricity, surged through me. I opened my mouth to speak and a strange language gushed forth.

Speaking a little Italian had been a part of me ever since babyhood and I'd been around people from all kinds of ethnic backgrounds, but I'd never heard words such as these that gushed from my mouth. To me it was a heavenly language. I knew from the warmth and love I was experiencing that I was communicating with my Lord.

No one else needed to understand. My life had undergone a complete transformation. *"Behold I make all things new"* became a scripture I embraced.

I wept for joy.

That night when I left I was still aware that I was going to prison, but the Lord Jesus who had wooed me and won me during that meeting would never leave me nor forsake me. He'd given me a new life. My past was forgiven. My very being exuded the peace I'd always sought. The King of Kings and Lord of Lords had given me a new life.

There was something else.

My grandfather came to America to escape the evil and corruption of his father back in Italy, but the curse followed him. He found himself just as deep in crime as his father had been. The curse followed my dad. It was now gone from me. That night when I accepted Jesus into my heart, our family curse was broken, never to return again.

In an instant my life was different.

I made a bunch of new friends who loved me as I was and praised God for my new life. I never experienced anything as powerful as I did that night. No adrenaline rush of my past could compare with the awesome presence of God through His Holy Spirit who swept me off my feet and molded me into a brand-new Rocco.

"Thank you, Jesus, for saving me!" I shouted.

My newly found brother and friend in Christ, Steve Totin, also received something that night. He said he was given a prophetic word about the two of us.

The Lord spoke to Steve's heart saying, "You will be with him for a long time."

Steve struggled with that, saying, "But, Lord, he's going to prison. I don't want to go to jail with this man."

Tony got saved too. God saved his soul and I saved his life. God spared us both.

The crew with us watched with amazement from a distance, astonished by what had just happened. This was the last thing they expected. No one could deny the power of God in that room.

Chapter 8

The Family Connection

P ower. Influence. Money. My Italian grandfather basked in their glory. He was a *respingente*—a buffer, a connector. He put people together. He connected warring Mafia people such as crime lords who needed to talk with their blood rivals, or ordinary people who needed to ask a favor.

My grandfather, Rocco Morelli, was a go-between, a legitimate businessman with impeccable old-country credentials. He knew who to approach and who owed whom.

My grandfather could be warm and loving. But he and his associates also could be cold and unfeeling. They could reward or punish.

With a steady hand, they ran New Kensington, Pennsylvania, our very own "Little Chicago."

Anyone traveling through my hometown in the 1960s would have had difficulty believing that our picturesque city was a Mafia hub.

Even someone fascinated with the mob would never have suspected that organized crime dominated this tranquil looking town near the Allegheny River, twenty miles north of Pittsburgh.

With its brick and frame homes on tree-lined streets, it appeared typically postwar. Yet, here my grandfather reigned in his own small gangsterland.

Gangsters ... the Mafia, the Mob, La Cosa Nostra, the words chill some souls.

But I grew up in it.

In the 1960s, Italian gangsters were my friends and mentors. In society, they still enjoyed a Jimmy Cagney romanticism— the thrill of murder and warm family ties, bootlegging and brotherhood, money laundering and *Mama Mia.*

The mystique of a closed society still intrigues some gawking outsiders. Perhaps it is because they can only glimpse our world through Mario Puzo novels, *Godfather* movies and tabloid newspaper sensationalism.

But numbers running and prostitution are not pretty. Neither is drug pushing or murder for hire. These are the livelihood of *la famiglia*—the family. They were the tricks of the trade of the underworld figures who were my heroes.

I inherited a legacy. They respected me because of it.

I was the Don's great-grandson.

Immense power and influence could become mine.

My fate was sealed shortly after my grandfather, Rocco, and my grandmother, Maria, immigrated to America from Italy in 1920.

Both were born into wealthy and powerful families. Her father had been Italy's Secretary of State. My grandfather's father, Don Francesco Morelli, had wielded tremendous political and social clout as the chief of the "carboneri," the corrupt Italian police.

But for people who were supposed to have such deep and meaningful family ties, there was a terrible shame and secrecy about our legacy, something of which my grandfather would rage in times of anger.

He was abandoned as a child. His powerful father turned his back on him and several of his other sons too. To our family's terrible humiliation, my great-grandfather put him up for adoption.

As a result, my grandfather was raised by a businessman and his wife. They sent him off to school to learn a trade. Their adopted son chose tailoring, learning to make custom-made suits of the finest linen and Italian silk. Some of his creations would be worn by the most notorious Mafia racketeers of his time.

Despite the shame, my grandfather talked about his father with pride:

"He'd cut your head off with a sword if you looked at him wrong!" My grandfather recalled.

Perhaps to pacify himself for shunning his sons, and so as not to sever family ties completely, the politically and socially powerful old man occasionally had his children brought to his castle on the sea on Sundays so they could visit their mother.

Perhaps in an effort to atone for his sins, he erected a chapel in his home by the sea and installed a fabulous church organ, the only one that existed in the area in those days.

My grandfather loved to listen to it. A talented musician, he also studied Italian opera and took up the tuba. Maybe he did it to please my great-grandfather, but the old man ignored him.

He never came to hear the boy perform.

In his old age, such bitter memories occasionally caused my grandfather's Italian temper to flare. I can still hear his rage as he talked about his father. Deep down I know he loved his father with all his heart and soul, but he was still hurting from the past.

My grandfather was a wonderful man. I loved him dearly. I remember his resounding voice booming out "O Solo Mio," coaching me to sing all the words in Italian. I also remember him trying to teach me entire operas echoing from his living room.

I adored my grandfather.

I recall him coldly telling me of his father, "I hated him!" I stared at him, spellbound.

"When I became a teenager," the old man told me, "he pursued me more than his other sons because he said he saw himself in me."

My grandfather paused, his gaze far away. "That made him all the more despicable. The last thing I wanted to be was like him."

He stared at me.

Although I was little, I understood. Or I thought I did. My grandfather told me how he had fled—eloping to America with my grandmother—just to spite the old man.

To infuriate him.

To get away from him.

The new immigrants were not alone, however. My grandfather brought other family members with him, which included a distant cousin, his wife and three sons. Two of those boys later became infamous mobsters—Sam and Kelly Mannarino, the other known as Jo-Joe was like "Alfredo" in the movie *The Godfather*, an outcast that was sent to Las Vegas.

Grandfather referred to all of them as his *compagni's*, family. I still remember them as men of honor who showed my grandfather great respect.

But, in America, instead of turning his back on the ways of his corrupt father, he became just like him.

In the novel *The Godfather*, Don Corleone was an olive oil merchant. In the same way, on the surface, my grandfather remained a master tailor by trade and then expanded into dry cleaning. But he was more than that. Far more.

My grandfather was a resource to many who sought his wisdom and his friendship. He was instrumental in forming the original Italian Club known today as the Sons of Italy which began as the Giuseppe Garibaldi Club, named after a famous general in Italy.

This fraternal organization became a social club for Italian Americans to gather together, which made it possible for the "boys" to operate a local gambling casino similar to those at Las Vegas.

My grandfather served as president of the Italian Club and became the Grand Venerable of the Sons of Italy Lodge in New Kensington. Today, the Sons of Italy is the largest Italian-American fraternal organization in the United States.

It is made up of members who are honest American citizens of Italian descent who hold the highest regard and respect for God, their family and their adopted country, the United States of America. My grandfather always said, "Put God first, then the family, then your work. Be fair and honest with all people, no matter what."

From places such as the club, Little Chicago began to grow to be a small but powerful empire of evil men who prospered even through the Great Depression.

I have been told that the word "Mafia" is derived from a word for "refuge" in Arab. The origins go back at least a thousand years when southern Spain and Italy were overrun by Moors— Muslim North Africans from Morocco, Tunisia and Algeria.

Italians needed places of refuge to escape the heavy oppression and taxation of their Arab invaders. So, they formed secret "refuge" societies or *Mafias.*

Although the Arabs were eventually thrown out, Italy was invaded many times over the next centuries. When the Normans invaded in the eleventh century, severe oppression returned. People were forced into labor on the large estates that the Norman rulers created. Once again, the only way to escape was to seek refuge.

During every subsequent invasion, the refuges established in earlier centuries were sought out again.

These secret societies, *these Mafias*, were mostly intended to unify people against their enemies. They created a sense of family based on ancestry and Italian heritage.

In the 1700s, Mafia members boldly sent pictures of a Black Hand to the wealthy landowners who had succeeded the foreign invaders and who were just as oppressive. It was extortion, a demand for money in return for "protection."

If the money wasn't paid, the recipients could expect violence such as kidnappings, bombings and murder.

By the 19th Century, the "Black Hand Society" grew larger and more criminally oriented. In 1876, Mafia Don Rafael Palizzolo ran for political office on the southern Italian Island of Sicily. He forced the voters to vote for him at gunpoint. After being elected, he promoted Mafia Don Crispi as Prime Minister. Together they put Sicily under Mafia control and funneled government funds to their society.

At the head of their organization stood local dons, or chiefs, who were in charge of Mafia chapters in every village.

Members were required to take an oath that included five basic principles.

1. A vow to honor the *omerta*, the tradition never to expose any Mafia secrets or members under penalty of death or torture.

2. Total obedience to the boss.

3. Assistance to any befriended Mafia faction, no questions asked.

4. Vengeance against any attack on members of the family, since an attack on one is an attack on all.

5. Avoid official contact with authorities.

By the nineteenth century, the Mafia had grown vast and strong. Whereas it had been a small partisan organization, it had turned into a large criminally oriented network, ignoring all forms of authority except its own.

When people from all over Europe started immigrating to America to find new and better opportunities, many Mafia members saw their chance to import their secret society to the United States.

In my grandfather's case, there was no conspiracy to bring the Mafia to Pennsylvania. When he eloped here with my grandmother, he had a trade; he was a fine tailor.

Upon arriving here, he was drawn to others who spoke Italian. Among them, he found friends and relatives with his same heritage. Many new arrivals such as my grandfather took up with people such as Vito Cascio Ferro. He fled to the United States in 1901 to escape arrest and formed the first recorded American Society of the Black Hand. Its members were hardened criminals and fugitives from southern Italy.

In 1924, Italian dictator Benito Mussolini was determined to rid Italy of the Mafia so many members fled to the United States to avoid persecution. This increased the numbers of members in the U.S. organizations.

These fleeing Italians were well aware there was money to be made in the United States through extortion, prostitution, gambling and bootlegging. Every large city soon had its own Mafia chapter.

When the Federal Government instituted Prohibition that banned the manufacturing and sale of alcoholic beverages, the Mafia saw an opportunity to make a great deal of money. Gangsters openly flaunted their wealth and power.

Among my grandfather's contemporaries was Charles Luciano who came to New York in 1906. He trained in the Five Points Gang, a Mafia crew, under John Torrio.

Luciano became friends with Al Capone and started his own prostitution racket in the early 1920s. He was in total control of prostitution in Manhattan by 1925.

In 1929 he was kidnapped, beaten and stabbed with an ice pick. He miraculously survived and maintained *"omerta."* By 1935, Luciano was known as The Boss of Bosses. He had previously established what the newspapers called "Murder, Inc."

Luciano's widespread criminal activities led to his being investigated by District Attorney Thomas E. Dewey. He was eventually sentenced to thirty to fifty years for extortion and prostitution. After his conviction, the United States government approached him with a deal. In exchange for his assistance in the Allied Invasion of Sicily, he was offered deportation to Rome. Luciano contacted his Mafia associates in Italy and the deal was made. The Allies successfully landed in Sicily without anything close to the loss of life suffered in the D-Day landings in France.

Another member of "Murder, Inc." was Benjamin (Bugsy) Siegel, who specialized in gambling and car theft as well as extorting money from movie studio owners, and demanding that Mafia characters in films be portrayed from a sympathetic perspective. His downfall came when he borrowed $5 million of syndicate money to build The Flamingo, the first large casino-hotel in Las Vegas.

Before it could become a money-maker, Luciano demanded repayment. Siegel refused, thinking he was as powerful as Luciano. Lucky Luciano then ordered Bugsy's death. Although Siegel was warned that a contract was out on his life, he continued to refuse to repay. On June 20, 1947, he was murdered.

Dutch Schultz, another major player in organized crime, opened an illegal "speakeasy" saloon in the Bronx borough of New York City during Prohibition and soon expanded to bootlegging, smuggling alcoholic beverages. Speakeasies were highly profitable businesses in those days.

During his trial for tax evasion, many of his rackets were taken over by Luciano, who expected Schultz to be convicted. Although this prompted him to move his operation to New Jersey, Schultz, who beat the tax charges, remained so influential, that Luciano brought him back into the New York operation.

Dewey, the mob-fighting District Attorney of New York, continued to pursue Schultz, who decided it was in his best interest to eliminate Dewey. The crime syndicate disagreed, fearing that the killing of such a popular prosecutor would only add to their problems. Schultz would not drop his plan. On the evening of October 23, 1935, while Schultz was setting up an ambush for Dewey, one of Luciano's hit men burst in and gunned down all of them, Schultz included.

Dewey went on to become the 1948 Republican candidate for President; narrowly losing to Harry S. Truman after all the pollsters proclaimed Dewey would win. Truman had entered politics in the good graces of the Kansas City Mafia, whereas Dewey was an ardent foe of the New York mob. Did the crime lords steal the election? Accusations continue to this day.

Alphonse "Scarface" Capone was another organizer of the early American Mafia. His involvement with organized crime began when he was eleven years old. As he got older, he graduated to the more powerful "Five Pointers Gang" where he became acquainted with Luciano.

When Johnny Torrio, the original leader of the "Five Pointers Gang" moved to Chicago, he invited Capone to be his sidekick.

Torrio's uncle, "Big Jim" Colisimo was the crime boss in Chicago. Trouble between uncle and nephew started, and Capone was hired to kill the uncle, leaving Torrio in charge of all Chicago. In 1925, when Torrio was severely wounded in a shoot out, he gave Capone his vast business empire, valued at $50 million a year. Capone fell out of favor with other Mafia gangsters, and several attempts were made on his life.

Capone took revenge by staging the infamous "St. Valentine's Day Massacre" in which he killed several of his enemies, ending resistance to his authority in Chicago. He was finally convicted for tax evasion and spent more than a decade at Alcatraz. In 1939 he was released from prison because he was in the advanced stages of syphilis, which had affected his mind, and eventually killed him in 1947.

The New York families first oversaw the city of Providence, Rhode Island, with its heavy Italian population, before the leadership came from Boston. The city became an important underworld power base after the emergence of Raymond Patriarca. The area and gang members operating there were considered by law enforcement officials as part of the Boston organized crime family. In the mid-1950s, when Patriarca took over the family leadership and ran his operations out of Providence, the criminal organization began to be referred to as the New England crime family.

Frank "Butsey" Morelli, one of five brothers, moved into New England from Brooklyn during World War I. Running his criminal operations from Rhode Island, he also controlled parts of Massachusetts, Connecticut and New Hampshire. Morelli maintained control of this area from 1917 to 1947 when he was dying of cancer. Morelli began to drink heavily and was loosing control of both his rackets and his men.

One of the things that got Morelli into trouble was his testimony before a grand jury in June 1947. Morelli was called to testify for harboring Doris Coppola, the wife of New York City mobster "Trigger Mike" Coppola, and her father. The two were on the run to avoid questioning about Coppola's participation in the November 1946 beating death of Joseph Scottoriggio, a Republican district captain. Joseph Lombardo, who was running the Boston family, put Philip Buccola in charge and allowed Morelli to die peacefully.

Prior to Morelli' s death in the early 1950s, Morelli said that his gang was responsible for the 1920 murders for which Nicola Sacco and Bartolomeo Vanzetti were executed. The trial of Sacco and Vanzetti for the double murder of two shoe company employees in South Braintree, Massachusetts drew national attention because the two were self-described anarchists who claimed they were being persecuted by the government.

Raymond Salvatore Loreda Patriarca was born in Worcester, Massachusetts on St. Patrick's Day, 1908. He was three years old when the family moved to Providence, Rhode Island where his father operated a liquor store. Patriarca's early life was uneventful until his father died in 1925. Just seventeen, Patriarca was arrested and convicted of breaking prohibition laws in Connecticut. Over the next thirteen years, his arrests included failing to stop for a policeman, breaking and entering, white slavery and masterminding a jailbreak in which a prison guard and a trusty were killed. During his lifetime, Patriarca was arrested or indicted twenty-eight times, convicted seven times, imprisoned four times, and served eleven years in prison. More than half of his prison time was for a murder conspiracy charge during the 1960s.

From an early age he possessed the right combination of brawn and brains that would make him successful in his chosen field. Patriarca gained a reputation for fairness, but if crossed he could be the most ruthless of men. He was once described by a Massachusetts State policeman as, "the toughest guy you ever saw."

During the Prohibition years, Patriarca served his apprenticeship in Providence, first as an associate and later as a member of the New York Mafia. In the late 1920s, he was involved with prostitution and hijacking.

In 1938, Patriarca participated in the robbery of a Brookline, Massachusetts, jewelry store. He was convicted of carrying a gun without a permit, possession of burglar's tools and armed robbery. He was sentenced for three to five years in the state prison. Less than three months into the sentence Patriarca was paroled setting off a political corruption storm in the wake of his release. The ensuing investigation lasted three years and in 1941 Daniel H. Coakley, a Massachusetts Governor's Councilor, was impeached and removed from office.

As Joseph Lombardo "replaced" Morelli with Buccola in 1947, Buccola controlled areas of New England until he fled in 1954 to Sicily leaving control of the family in the hands of Patriarca.

After getting out of prison in 1938, Patriarca returned to Providence where his influence and power increased during the 1940s. During this period he became the driving force behind what would become the New England Crime Family. By the early 1950s, it was impossible to be a major figure in crime in New England and not have to deal with Patriarca.

His rise included murder and building political influence. Patriarca's only rival in Providence was Irishman Carlton O'Brien, a former bootlegger who went into gambling and took control of the race-wire service. Patriarca's men shot O'Brien to death in 1952.

Records from illegal FBI bugs placed in Patriarca's office from 1962 to 1965 indicate many political payoffs to the governor's office, legislators and judges in both Rhode Island and Massachusetts; authorities later said that his political contacts did not yield much. He once tried to use these connections to get Larry Zannino, one of his top lieutenants, paroled from prison but failed.

When the Kefauver hearings began in 1950, the old-time leadership in Boston was in fear that the publicity might expose them and their operations. Lombardo ordered all bookmaking operations shut down, or to operate without a central lay off bank and without police protection. During the Kefauver threat, the bookmakers lost Lombardo's protection service, but gained more freedom to operate. This overreaction to the Kefauver hearings, which never materialized in Boston, opened the door for Gennaro Angiulo to move in on the gambling operations in the city.

By the late 1950s, Angiulo was being shaken down regularly by mob heavies in Boston because he was not a made member of the family. Angiulo solved this problem by taking $50,000 down to Patriarca in Providence and promising him an additional $100,000 a year. These payments led to Angiulo becoming a made member of the family without having to "make his bones" as other members were required. The Patriarca/Angiulo relationship was strictly financial. Angiulo was never well liked or respected, but as long as he kept the money flowing into Providence, he had the backing and protection of Patriarca.

With the retirement of Buccola in 1954, Providence became the center of the New England Family's operations. From a wood-frame, two-story building in Providence, Patriarca kept his office and ran his crime empire. The building housed the National Cigarette Service Company and Coin-O-Matic Distributors, a vending machine and pinball business, on Atwell Avenue on what is called Federal Hill. Made members of organized crime there were called "members of the Office." Atwell was a noisy open-air market, which was also an armed camp with "spotters" located everywhere. This set up was very similar to other popular mob-run areas like Mulberry Street in Manhattan's Little Italy, Arthur Avenue in the Bronx, and Prince Street in Boston.

Patriarca had a "polished way" with the police and the public. From his Atwell Avenue office, he held court and sorted out both domestic and crime family disputes.

Patriarca was involved in a complex maze of interests. He completely controlled some markets, especially those involving gambling, loan-sharking, and pornography, and dabbled in others such as truck hijacking and drug traffic, in which free-lancers negotiated a fee to do business. However, Patriarca had a hard and fast rule on narcotics and there was nothing worse than dealing in drugs as far as the boss was concerned. He said there was no reason for gang members to be dealing. No one in the New England mob ever starved, whether they were made guys or working for the organization. Patriarca wasn't like Genovese or old Joe Profaci. He made sure his men got paid well.

Over the years, Patriarca built a relationship with the New York Genovese and Profaci/Colombo Crime Families. The New York families in the past had exercised control over Providence, and Patriarca was considered their man.

Patriarca' s underboss, Henry Tameleo, was a member of the Bonanno Crime Family. Part of Patriarca's dealings with the Genovese Family was over territorial matters with the New England Family. The Connecticut River was considered the dividing line between the New York and New England Families. The Genovese Family exercised control in Hartford, Springfield, and Albany, while the cities of Worcester and Boston, as well as the state of Maine were under New England.

Patriarca was a member of the ruling Mafia commission in New York. He also had some national investments, holding hidden interests in two Las Vegas casinos and pieces of deals in Florida and Philadelphia.

Grandfather Rocco (middle) with his paisans *(friends)*
after they came to the US from Italy.

Rocco and Maria, Rocco's grandparents, in front of fountain at Saint Peter's Square in Rome, before having an audience with Pope Pius XII (1947).

Grandfather Rocco Morelli

The Mob lays to rest one of its own. Grandfather Rocco watches the pallbearers from the doorway of the church (top middle).

Grandfather Rocco at his home in New Kensington, PA.

November 1970 – Grandfather Rocco and Grandmother Maria's 50th Wedding Anniversary at the Sons of Italy Club in New Kensington, PA.

November 1980 – Grandfather Rocco and Grandmother Maria's 60th Wedding Anniversary at Tambellini's Italian Restaurant in Pittsburgh PA.

Hugo in the U.S. Army during the Korean Conflict.

Hugo (middle) with his Army buddies on leave.

Hugo and Mary Morelli, Rocco's parents –
Married on June 30, 1956.

Hugo and Mary arrive at the Sons of Italy Club
in New Kensington, PA., for their wedding reception.

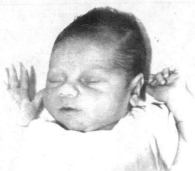

Baby Rocco
Born December 4, 1959
at Pittsburgh Hospital

Rocco's first crew cut

Rocco at 18 months

Rocco's first dance with Susie the Doll

Rocco with his Grandma Anna and mother Mary.
Anna is Mary's mother. Christmas 1967

Rocco with his mom and dad
after his first Holy Communion in the Catholic Church.

Rocco with his dad Hugo (left) and uncle Eddie at the farm.

*Rocco, at 17, jamming on his guitar
leaving for a gig with his band "Stardust."*

Rocco and his band "Stardust."

Rocco's graduation picture –
Class of 1977.

Rocco at age 19 as a police officer
in Westmoreland County Police Department.

*Rocco with Grandfather Rocco and Grandmother Maria
in their la cucina (kitchen).*

*Rocco at Tony's mom's Pasta Palace,
one of his old meeting places and favorite places to eat.*

Rocco's dad Hugo and Grandfather Rocco.

*Mom and Dad's
50th Wedding
Anniversary
June 30, 2006.*

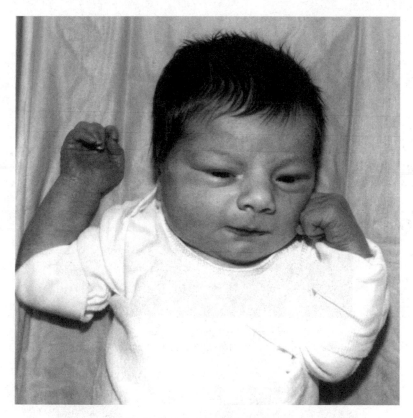

Racquel Morelli, Rocco's baby girl, born December 10, 1984.
A precious gift from God.

Rocco with
Grandfather Rocco
holding daughter
Racquel at her
Baptismal Celebration
Dinner.

Christmas at the Penitentiary in 1987.
Mom and Dad were always there for family visits.

Mom, Dad, and daughter Racquel, who just woke up from a nap after the
drive in the car to see her daddy who was away at college (prison).

Mug shot of Rocco and Christine. FBI Chicago's most wanted. Valentine's Day at Al Capone's Dinner Show in Kissimmee, Florida.

Another day at "School" (prison). Rocco with his little girl Racquel on visitation day in prison.

Rocco and Christine wed on Christmas Eve 1996. Christine, Racquel, and Rocco at the wedding reception.

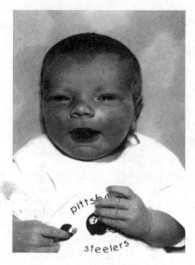

Rocco's grandson, Johnny.
Ready to try out
for the Steelers.
Born August 15, 2004.

Rocco's grandson, Johnny,
one year old.

Rocco and Christine – Carnival Cruise 2004.

Rocco ministering in a state prison with
Operation Starting Line – Prison Fellowship.

Rocco ministering at a County Boot Camp
with Youth for Christ Ministries.

Rocco ministering in Africa.

Rocco was part of the team at Prison Fellowship Ministries. He's shown here with ministry founder Chuck Colson.

"Rocco is an immediate impact everywhere he speaks. His message is inspiring as well as motivating. He is truly an asset to any event."
— *Melvin Adams, Former Harlem Globetrotter and Pro Basketball Player.*

Chapter 9

The Family vs. The FBI

In the wake of the Apalachin Summit, the FBI began their pursuit of organized crime in earnest. When Robert Kennedy became Attorney General, he launched an aggressive program to place listening devices in as many mob-meeting places as possible. Agents also worked at developing informants within the ranks of organized crime.

One of the criminals they eventually turned was New England Family associate Joseph Barboza. Nicknamed "The Animal," Barboza was born to Portuguese parents in 1932 in New Bedford, Massachusetts. He became a cold-blooded killer who claimed to have murdered twenty-six men. Barboza would become known as the Joe Valachi of the New England Family.

In trouble since the age of twelve, he was in and out of reformatories and prisons before hooking up with the mob in 1958. By 1966, Barboza had worn out his welcome with organized crime. In October he was arrested in Boston's infamous "Combat Zone" on a concealed weapons charge and bond was set at $100,000. Barboza grew concerned when his bail wasn't furnished by either Patriarca or Angiulo.

Five weeks later, Barboza still languished in jail as two friends tried to scrape together money to get him released. Arthur "Tash" Bratsos and Thomas J. DePrisco, Jr. had collected $59,000. In November they visited the "Nite Lite Cafe," managed by "Ralphie Chang" Lamattina, to do a little fund-raising. Both men were shot to death and dumped in South Boston to make it look like a rival Irish gang murdered them.

Not only were Barboza's two pals dead, but the $59,000 was missing too.

The FBI began diligent efforts to turn Barboza. In December, Joe Amico, another friend of Barboza's, was murdered. The following month, after a ten-day trial, Barboza was sentenced to a five-year term at Walpole on the weapons charges. In June 1967, Barboza started talking. Patriarca and Tameleo were indicted on June 20 for conspiracy to kill for the 1966 murder of Providence bookmaker Willie Marfeo. Two months later Angiulo was accused of participating in the murder of Rocco DiSeglio. Finally in October, Tameleo and Peter Limone, an Angiulo bodyguard, were charged with the March 1965 murder of Edward "Teddy" Deegan.

In the first trial, Angiulo was found not guilty after a jury deliberated for less than two hours. None of the jurors had found Barboza believable. The second trial, however, had a different outcome. Patriarca was found guilty of conspiracy to kill Willie Marfeo who was murdered by four shotgun blasts in a telephone booth at a Federal Hill restaurant.

While the trials were going on, the mob tried to get at Barboza by planting a bomb in the car of his attorney, John Fitzgerald. The blast resulted in Fitzgerald losing his right leg below the knee. The FBI kept Barboza on the move to prevent the mob from finding him. One of the hiding places was an officer's quarters located at Fort Knox. In May 1968, the Deegan trial began. After fifty days of testimony and deliberations, the jury returned a guilty verdict.

Barboza had done an impressive job. Of the three trials at which he testified, two ended in guilty verdicts resulting in four gang members on death row, two in prison for life, and Patriarca on his way to the Atlanta Federal Penitentiary.

For his testimony, Barboza was given a one-year prison term, including time served. He was paroled in March 1969 and told to leave Massachusetts forever. In 1971, he pleaded guilty to a second-degree murder charge in California and sentenced to five years at Folsom Prison. Less than three months after his release he was murdered in San Francisco by Joseph "J.R." Russo on February 11, 1976.

Raymond Patriarca began his prison term in March 1969. While serving time, he received a ten-year sentence from Rhode Island for conspiring to kill Willie Marfeo's brother, Rudolph, and Anthony Melei. Both were shot gunned to death on April 20, 1968 in Providence. Patriarca completed his federal sentence in April 1973 and was transferred to a Rhode Island prison where he remained until paroled on January 9, 1975. During the six years Patriarca was behind bars he continued to run his crime family from prison.

Charges continued to plague Patriarca for the rest of his life. In 1978, Vincent Teresa testified that he was present in 1960 when the CIA gave the mob a four million dollar contract to murder Cuban leader Fidel Castro. Teresa stated that Patriarca helped select Maurice (Pro) Werner, a Brookline, Massachusetts convict to kill Castro, but the plot was never carried out. In December 1983, Patriarca was charged with ordering the 1965 murder of Raymond "Baby" Curcio. The murder was in response to Curcio and Teresa burglarizing the home of Patriarca's brother Joseph. Finally on March 13, 1984, Patriarca was arrested while in the hospital for ordering the 1968 murder of bank robber Robert Candos. Patriarca believed Candos was going to testify against him.

Raymond Patriarca died on July 11, 1984 after suffering a heart attack at the home of a girlfriend. He was 76 years old.

On September 19, 1983, FBI agents arrested Jerry Angiulo, three of his brothers and two other associates in a Boston Restaurant. In the wake of Patriarca's death in 1984, Angiulo, although still in jail awaiting trail, was hoping to succeed to the top spot. It was not to be. Disliked in Providence, Angiulo was demoted to a mere soldier when top lieutenant, Larry Zannino, threw his support behind the late mob boss's son, Raymond J. "Junior" Patriarca. One Providence police official stated, "If that job had gone to Jerry Angiulo, we would have bodies all over the place."

According to the Boston newspapers, the national commission had to approve Junior's ascendancy, which they did in early 1985. Patriarca quickly rewarded Zannino for his backing by appointing him consigliere. In early May 1985, Zannino was ordered jailed by a United States Magistrate. Over the next two years Zannino feigned health problems to keep from going to trial. When he was finally ordered to appear in 1987, he was found guilty. Sentenced to thirty years in prison, he died there on March 6, 1996.

In August 1985, another of the old-timers passed away. Henry Tameleo died in prison of respiratory failure. He had served seventeen years of a life sentence for his role in the Deegan murder. At the time, Tameleo was looking forward to a December parole date. He died the oldest inmate in the Massachusetts prison system at age eighty-four.

On February 26, 1986, Gennaro Angiulo, two of his brothers and an associate were convicted on the 1983 racketeering charges. Angiulo, who had been in prison since the indictment, was sentenced to forty-five years in prison and fined $120,000.

With Angiulo in prison, the role of underboss went to Francesco "Paul" Intiso. A contemporary and friend of the elder

Patriarca, Intiso served as a kind of caretaker until his death in 1985. His role as underboss, according to authorities, was filled by William P. "The Wild Man" Grasso of New Haven, Connecticut. Grasso had a close working relationship with the crime families of New York. Some crime authorities believe the underboss position went to seventy year old Charles Quintino of Revere, Massachusetts because Junior needed someone closer to home to oversee the Boston operations. One of the capos in the new regime was Joseph "J.R." Russo, the assassin of Joe Barboza. Russo had assumed control of the East Boston-Revere area.

The leadership abilities of Junior Patriarca were in question by law enforcement experts. Some experts believed that Grasso, with his New York City connections, was the real power in New England. If he was, his reign was short lived. On June 16, 1989, the sixty-two year old Grasso was found along the banks of the Connecticut River with a bullet in the back of his head.

In the aftermath of the Grasso murder, Nicholas "Nicky" Bianco of Providence was considered by the FBI the "unofficial" head of the Providence operations with Junior serving as a titular head. Also continuing to rise in 1989 was J.R. Russo. The same day Grasso was found dead, Frances P. "Cadillac Frank" Salemme was shot and seriously wounded in Saugus, Massachusetts. Russo's step brother Robert 'Bobby Russo" Carrozza was suspected in the shooting.

On March 26, 1990, Junior Patriarca and twenty reputed family members were indicted on charges that included racketeering, gambling, extortion, drug trafficking and murder. The RICO (Racketeer Influenced and Corrupt Organizations Act) indictment named Bianco as the underboss of the family, and J.R. Russo as the consigliere. In addition, five capos or lieutenants were also charged; Biagio DiGiacomo, Vincent M. "The Animal" Ferrara, Matthew L. Guglielmetti, Dennis D. "Champagne" Lepore and the aforementioned Carrozza. The twenty-one arrests included family members in Connecticut, Massachusetts, and Rhode Island. The charges were described as the "most sweeping attack ever launched on a single organized crime family," and capped a five-year investigation.

The indictment contained charges against seventeen family members who were present at a Mafia induction ceremony held for four men in Medford, Massachusetts on October 29, 1989. It was the first time members of law enforcement were able to tape a family initiation ceremony which crime family members had denied for years ever took place. The taping of the ceremony created much embarrassment for the New England Family; it would be used at other trials for years to prove the existence of a secret criminal society.

In early February 1991, the *Boston Globe* reported that due to the embarrassment caused by the tapes, Bianco replaced Junior Patriarca as head of the New England Family. Bianco was described as low-key, secretive, private and "anything but flashy."

At the time, a former Rhode Island State Police investigator stated that Junior Patriarca "Didn't have the brains or the power to lead the family. He couldn't lead a Brownie troop." The paper also reported that the recently wounded Salemme of Sharon, Massachusetts had become underboss.

Bianco, who grew up on Atwell Avenue, was originally with the Colombo Crime Family in New York before serving the elder Patriarca for three decades. Described as a "strong player in the New England underworld for decades," Bianco waited patiently to become boss. He helped run the family in the early 1970s during the critical period the elder Patriarca was serving time. Bianco moved up the ranks quietly, never attracting attention. His low-key image caused some members of the Boston mob to complain that they didn't know what he looked like.

Law enforcement figures stated that because of his insulated life-styles and practices they were never able to record him on tape. During the 1960s, Bianco was the liaison between the New England Family and the Colombo Family. Bianco lived in Barrington, Rhode Island, a wealthy town southeast of Providence. His children attended private schools, and one son went on to law school. In 1984, Bianco was acquitted of murder conspiracy charges in the death of Anthony Mirabella. A year later, similar charges against him in the murder of Richard Callei were dismissed.

When the RICO trials finally got underway, John F. "Sonny" Castagna, an associate of the Patriarca Family, revealed that Patriarca Junior would be killed by Boston mobsters if he did not step down. Castagna, testifying in May 1991, said the story was relayed to him by J.R. Russo: "Raymond Junior, with tears in his eyes, begged for his life." The testimony took place during the Hartford trial which included defendant Gaetano Milano, who Castagna, now in the Federal Witness Protection Program with his son Jack Johns, claimed murdered William Grasso.

The Hartford trial came to an end on August 8, 1991 with eight members of the Patriarca Family convicted of violating the RICO Act. Bianco and Americo Petrillo were both convicted on two counts of racketeering. Milano was found guilty of murdering Grasso. Frank Colantoni, Jr., and brothers Frank and Louis Pugliano were found guilty of conspiracy, in the Grasso murder. The other two defendants, found guilty of racketeering, were Salvatore "Butch" D'Aquila, Jr., and Louis Faillia.

On November 25, Bianco was sentenced to eleven years, five months in prison and fined $125,000. He was ordered to report on December 30. Three years later, at the age of sixty-two, he died in a federal prison in Springfield, Missouri. He suffered from Lou Gehrig's disease.

On December 3, 1991 Raymond J. Patriarca pleaded guilty to racketeering and other charges in Boston, disassociating himself from several codefendants charged with more serious crimes. Prosecutors tried in vain to have a long sentence imposed on Junior Patriarca. Part of the pre-sentencing testimony came from a former Philadelphia mobster, Scarfo Family underboss Philip Leonetti, who was now working with the government.

In June 1992, Patriarca was sentenced to eight years, one month. His legal woes continued over the next few years. The United States Court of Appeals ruled that a federal judge erred in his sentencing of Junior. The court claimed the judge did not consider if Patriarca was responsible for crimes committed by his crime family members. As a result of the ruling, an additional twenty-three months were tacked on to his sentence.

The Boston RICO trial was set to get underway with jury selection on January 6, 1992. Sixteen days later, all of the defendants entered guilty pleas on the condition that they were allowed to deny they were members of the Mafia, La Cosa Nostra or the Patriarca crime family. The men were fined and sentenced on April 29. J.R. Russo was fined $758,000 and sentenced to sixteen years. Vincent Ferrara was fined $1,116,000 and sentenced to twenty-two years. Robert "Bobby Russo" Carrozza was fined $878,000 and sentenced to nineteen years. Dennis Lepore was fined $767,000 and sentenced to fourteen years. Finally, Carmen Tortora was fined $2,000 and sentenced to thirteen years.

The pleas also protected Ferrara, Russo and Carrozza from prosecution in the murder of Grasso and the attempted murder of Frank Salemme. Ferrara was also protected from prosecution in the 1985 slaying of Vincent James Limoli. J.R. Russo, whose indictment included the 1976 murder of Joe Barboza, told the court, "I understand there is enough evidence to prove me guilty (of the Barboza murder), but I am not admitting to guilt." On June 1, 1998, Russo died in the same Missouri prison as Nicholas Bianco.

Chapter 10

"Little Chicago"
The New Kensington/Pittsburgh Family

M y grandfather rose to power amid all this. He watched the American Mafia turn into something completely different than the secret societies back in Italy. The European Mafia was founded on a sense of loyalty and respect for culture, family and heritage. Its purpose was to protect its members' interests and provide them success in business in exchange for absolute loyalty and submission to the will of the local Don.

Our family's faction of the mob rose up in the 1920s around Don Stefano Monastero, who was successful in the usual mob rackets like protection, gambling and bootlegging. Joseph Siragusa succeeded Monastero in Pittsburgh and was the boss from 1929 until 1931, when he was murdered because of his close association with New York City mobster Salvatore Maranzano, who had been killed three days earlier.

John Bazzano took over in 1931 and organized a rather unorganized family. On August 8, 1932 in the middle of a Brooklyn street his body was found strangled and stabbed to death and sewn into a burlap sack. Bazzano was reportedly murdered when called to New York City to explain the slayings of the three Volpe brothers. He replied that what he did in Pittsburgh was no concern to anyone else in the organization.

Vincenzo Capizzi was the family's head from 1933 until 1937. Capizzi was the first boss to bring national attention to the Pittsburgh family. He was the one who put the Pittsburgh mob on the map. At the time, Pittsburgh was one of the fastest growing cities in the country. The Italian-American population in Pittsburgh in the 1940 census ranked Pittsburgh third behind Chicago and New York.

Capizzi's successor was Frank Amato. Amato was the boss until 1956. During his reign, he tried to infiltrate the steelworkers' unions. Various factors and frequent changes in leadership resulted in close ties with the Genovese family—on whom the movies *The Godfather* are allegedly based.

John LaRocca took control of the family in 1956 and was thrown into the spotlight. The long tradition of secrecy about the Pittsburgh mob was over. The FBI kept closer tabs on the family under his reign. John LaRocca died in 1986, having a long reign, and like many other Pittsburgh bosses, untouched by the law.

One FBI report in 1985 said that the Pittsburgh family ranked in the lower echelon of the Mafia across the country. However, a 1995 FBI report stated that the top families had been sharply hit with prosecutions during the 1990s, including the families in New York City, Philadelphia, Chicago, Buffalo, Boston and Pittsburgh.

My grandfather dealt with them all. He was a go-between— an intermediary between the families.

Gabriel "Kelly" and Sam Mannarinos' Pittsburgh Mafia legacy consists of far more than a handful of gangster stories. In November 1957, New Kensington's Gabriel "Kelly" Mannarino had just made national headlines as one the gangsters rounded up at a national Mafia conclave in Apalachin, N.Y.

For more than forty years—from the "glory days" of the 1940s and 1950s when the Mannarinos controlled the New

Kensington gambling rackets through the conviction in the early 1980s of reputed family associate and Arnold drug trafficker Gary Golden—the Pittsburgh family has written parts of the Valley's criminal history.

Kelly Mannarino's reign over local organized crime ended on July 15, 1980, four days after his death. Pastor Francis Ginocchi, at Mount St. Peter Catholic Church, delivered a flowery eulogy praising Mannarino's civic concern and generosity.

Three years later he had to defend the eulogy in a story marking his retirement: "All I said was that this man was always ready to help," Ginocchi said. "If anyone was going to judge him, let God do it."

Try as they might, federal and state investigators never had much success pinning the rackets label to Kelly Mannarino, or his older brother, Sam. In fact, the best investigators ever did was to manage a penny-ante conviction against Sam in 1963.

That case involved skimming profits from the brothers' NuKen Novelty pinball machine collections in 1957 and 1958. Sam got three years probation in that case, but Kelly was acquitted, although he had close calls in other federal cases in 1957 and 1969.

In 1969, Kelly was indicted in a Teamsters Union kickback scheme. Also indicted were then-Pittsburgh mob boss Sebastian John LaRocca and Frank Amato Sr.—Kelly's father-in-law and LaRocca's second-in-command.

All were acquitted on charges that they mediated a dispute over which two of several Mafia families would have jurisdiction over the kickbacks.

In 1957, Kelly was acquitted of offering a witness $150 to "keep his mouth shut" during a vote fraud trial in 1956.

Three other people, John Fontana, Mike Sicilia and Frank Phillips, all of New Kensington, were convicted of masterminding a ballot-box stuffing scheme during the city's 1952 elections.

The trio was convicted during the new trial in which authorities said Kelly bribed Harry W. Truitt Jr.—a dental assistant with known Communist links.

Kelly was acquitted after his defense attorneys produced a string of civic leaders who testified against Truitt's character and political beliefs.

The irony of that victory became apparent in 1958 when the Mannarinos were linked—but not indicted—for running guns to Fidel Castro's Cuban rebels. Authorities said the Mannarinos backed Castro—the Communist—over Fulgencia Batista when the government seized the Mannarino's Sans Soucie gambling casino in Havana three years earlier.

Daniel "Speedo" Hanna's colorful criminal roots as a Mannarino strong-arm include his conviction for trying to ship $10,000 worth of weapons stolen from an Ohio National Guard armory to Fidel Castro's rebel soldiers.

Although the Mannarinos never were indicted, authorities said the scheme was an attempt to aid Castro who, it was thought, would have protected the Mannarinos' reputed Cuban gambling interests.

The fact that Hanna delivered the guns to the airport in a delivery truck owned by Sam Mannarino lent credence to that scenario as did Cuban politics in the 1950s.

Among the others convicted in the gunrunning attempt were Rothman, Sam Mannarino's son-in-law, Victor Carlucci, and New Kensington gambler and Bachelor's Club operator Joseph "Red" Giordano.

Hanna's "Cuban guns" link was sufficient to make him a target of a 1958 federal racketeering probe. Hanna and reputed Pittsburgh family member Thomas "Sonny" Ciancutti, were named as associates of the Mannarinos and John Fontana when called before a federal grand jury.

Fontana was considered Kelly Mannarino's "right hand man" in the New Kensington rackets, according to federal authorities.

Once again, the federal probe made for good reading but not much else. Instead, authorities and the few private citizens like Eugene Simon who pursued the Mannarinos had to be content with a string of moral victories.

"I've always said that the problem was not so much the bad guys as the good guys who wouldn't stand up and be counted," Simon said.

In the mid-1950s, Simon and others challenged a Mannarino-backed move to replace electronic voting machines with paper ballots ostensibly because they were easier to tamper with.

The Pennsylvania Supreme Court rejected the Mannarino initiative six to nothing.

In the early 1960s, Attorney General Robert Kennedy intensified his high-profile war on the Mannarinos in the Valley. But the spectacular federal raids never really hurt the Mannarinos personally, though they did disrupt district rackets operations.

Despite such dramatic-sounding efforts, Kelly Mannarino had only two arrests for minor gambling charges early in his career, and a liquor law violation stemming from the operation of his Cuban gambling casino in the 1950s.

The early 1960s brought increased notoriety for the Mannarinos and anxious times for local officials. City fathers tried desperately to downplay the rackets, which were becoming a source of municipal embarrassment.

Coupled with reports of the Mannarino's former Cuban gambling holdings, Kelly's suntanned skin and reported regular mob junkets to Florida, these official disclaimers drew snickers of public disbelief. Still, there was relatively little public outcry during the Mannarinos' heyday because their successes coincided with the Valley's prosperous postwar boom.

In fact, many officials saw the Mannarinos almost as benefactors—godfathers who kept the Valley streets free from the specter of drugs. "The people who were out here in the 1960s would never have tolerated the narcotics," said former Mayor DeMao of the Mannarinos.

Adding to the Mannarinos' public stability, if not respectability, was a series of business partnerships they had nurtured. They owned the NuKen Novelty Co., S&S Vending and Catoris Candy Inc. Crime commission surveillance indicates the candy company was probably used as a base of operations.

Kelly Mannarino's Family Drive-In Theater, Inc. owned several other real estate holdings. Those holdings included the location of the New Kensington police substation.

DeMao said he knew only one side of the Mannarinos. "People like me never knew their problems, the mechanics of their business. We knew them as respectable businessmen."

DeMao painted the Mannarinos as benign civic custodians who kept the area clean in return for being left alone to concentrate on running the area's gambling rackets.

In excusing the gambling rackets, DeMao said: "It's a harmless vice."

Even Pennsylvania Crime Commission field agent Mokos was sympathetic to the notion that gambling is a victimless crime. But he wasn't sold on the side effects of such operations, most notably, political corruption. Political corruption is a given wherever illegal gambling is rampant.

"It's not gambling that's the problem. It's what control gambling has over the government." Mokos said. "It's also our feeling that any larger organized gambling's (profits) will be used for narcotics."

Although the Mannarinos enjoyed the "drug-free" reputation attributed to the rest of the Amato/LaRocca family, Mokos said any such claims are untrue, or at best hypocritical.

"As far as the whole narcotics thing, the family leaders, like LaRocca and Genovese, it was something they didn't want to get involved in but they knew it had to be done as far as the money was concerned," Mokos said. "So they looked the other way and said if you do it, we don't want to see it." Mokos noted, however, that the bosses likely received their fair share of drug proceeds.

The money to be made from drugs, and the greed associated with it, filtered down through family ranks.

Because the Mannarinos never were publicly linked to drugs, the role of the mob in the Valley drug trade was unclear.

Ben Beal, who covered the Mannarinos' 1963 pinball skimming trial, said the Mannarinos at least knew of such traffic. "I went to lunch with them one day during a trial recess, and Sam said, 'Yeah, we know it's coming in, and if we see any of those guys, we'll kill'em,'" Beal said.

But Sam never said they weren't involved. They just didn't want it in their own backyard.

Indicted in 1958 by the grand jury was Samuel J. Lanzino Sr., charged with running the Mannarino numbers bank. He continued to be connected to criminal activity into the 1980s and pleaded guilty in 1989 to poolselling and bookmaking. The Lanzino arrest was a spin-off of the Hatzimbes numbers investigation.

Also arrested in a spin-off investigation were Charles "Chuckie" Mercurio, and father Peter Mercurio Sr., as well as my very own father, Hugo Morelli, as part of the alleged Hatzimbes number ring.

Peter Mercurio was a partner with Hatzimbes in the after-hours Aluminum City Club — formerly known as St. Anthony's or "Saint A's" — in New Kensington, a place of refuge for many of us in those days.

Criminals who work with (but are not members of) the Mafia are called associates. They usually pay the Mafia for protection from police or other criminals.

U.S. Attorney Thomas Corbett linked the Pittsburgh mob to the Hatzimbes gambling ring. The arrests were discussed by mob figures while under FBI surveillance.

The Pennsylvania Crime Commission presumed that the Hatzimbes ring had to split part of its profits with the mob to keep operating. The commission considered Saint A's as a former hot spot where Golden ran gambling operations, and charged that Golden ran similar operations in the past, most notably at the defunct Westmoreland Club in New Kensington, for his first cousin, Ciancutti.

Ciancutti ran New Kensington area rackets as a member of the Pittsburgh family after Kelly Mannarino's death.

Both Golden and Ciancutti were being watched closely by authorities as the Mannarino legacy spun into the 1990s.

The exact nature of the Ciancutti / Golden link was foggy because Golden's primary business—drugs—flies in the face of Ciancutti's public reputation as an old-style mobster who deplores drug traffic. Also, Ciancutti has never been charged with drug trafficking, although his name has been linked to drugs in area trials.

In 1986 ex-FBI agent Dan Metrione said Ciancutti and Golden bought cocaine from Eugene "Nick the Blade" Gesuale, a convicted drug runner and associate of Charles "Chuckie" Porter.

Porter, thought to be a *caporegime* or at least an influential Mafia family member, was the focus of Pittsburgh's rackets trial. On the other hand, Golden, following his 1983 drug conviction, stressed Ciancutti's noninvolvement in drugs.

Ultimately, the crime commission doesn't recognize Ciancutti as a drug figure. Whether he knew what Golden was doing is another thing, but the commission hasn't come up with anything to link Ciancutti to Golden's operation.

The commission has, however, linked Ciancutti to high-level mob dealings since 1969, about the same time that Golden became known to the crime commission. In that year, Ciancutti accompanied then family boss Sebastian John LaRocca and Kelly Mannarino to a national mob meeting to discuss a successor to New York crime boss Vito Genovese. Since then, the commission has linked Ciancutti to a 1980 meeting in Youngstown, Ohio.

Ciancutti and Mannarino made the trip at LaRocca's request to speak with warring members of that city's mob.

By 1980, Golden, too, had attained a higher profile in the crime commission's reports. From 1969 to 1974 he reportedly operated the Luv-In nightclub in Pittsburgh and was arrested for keeping a gambling house at the Arnold Pool Hall in 1970.

Relatively minor brushes with the law continued, including a 1972 arrest for possession of dynamite, which was not pursued after a search warrant was ruled illegal, and a 1976 conviction for selling marijuana, which was reversed on appeal in 1981.

Golden also was charged in a 1979 drug raid that netted several hundred pounds of cocaine, but charges were dismissed when the search yielding the evidence was ruled illegal. Throughout this period, Golden was linked to Ciancutti by the crime commission.

In 1969, Charles R. Ligoon, formerly of New Kensington, pleaded guilty to poolselling and bookmaking at 1717 Fifth Avenue—a building owned by Golden.

In 1977, Ligoon became an employee of Ciancutti's at S&S Vending Co., formerly owned by Kelly Mannarino. Ligoon was a well-known gambler who frequented the Westmoreland Club, which Golden managed for Ciancutti, according to the crime commission.

The commission said a theft ring allegedly fenced goods at the club in 1978 and 1979 through a man named Leo Sussman. Telephone records from Sussman's address showed frequent calls to a pay phone registered in Ciancutti's name at the Westmoreland Club in the spring of 1978.

This was "Little Chicago."

"Little Chicago" Today.

Captain Jack Plaisted of the Butler police was surprised when a pistol reported stolen in the city turned up less than two months later in an attempted homicide in Austin, Texas.

"Then I learned that drugs were involved," he said.

For police, it was just another case of the long reach now seen in the drug and gun trade. Increasingly, investigators say, the so-called "local drug dealer" is becoming a thing of the past.

In the Valley and surrounding region, even street-level dealers travel widely. From the inner city to rural country roads and across state lines, drug dealers are expanding their territories and client bases.

Valley and outside traffickers sell heroin, crack and other drugs along city streets and in suburbs and rural areas, and they steal, trade and sell guns.

Users steal from friends and family, and break into stores and houses for money or anything that can be sold for quick cash. They also trade guns or sex to get drugs.

Increasingly, Valley traffickers—mostly a loose confederation of people who sometimes work together—are buying and selling drugs well outside of their home territories. If the dealers had a single business card, it might very well read, "Have drugs, will travel" and give a cell-phone number or e-mail address.

During a sixteen-month study, reporters from the *Valley News Dispatch* in New Kensington talked with addicts, counselors, police officers, federal agents and drug-trend analysts to ask about homegrown traffickers who, at times, do business throughout the country.

According to police and court records, the desire for more money sends small-town dealers throughout the Valley, plus places such as Philadelphia, New York, Texas, Arizona and parts of West Virginia, Ohio, and sections of Pittsburgh known for drugs and guns. If the risk is right, dealers will travel hundreds of miles, or send assistants, to buy from suppliers.

On March 14, 2001, a Butler man told police someone took his .40-caliber semiautomatic pistol. Federal agents believe the gun likely was taken to Pittsburgh or somewhere in the Valley before it was used in the Austin shooting.

The victim, a reputed Austin drug dealer, survived. Two men, one from Austin and the other from New Kensington, with close ties to the Valley were charged with trying to kill him when he refused to buy drugs from them.

A witness told police an Arnold woman and her associate from New Kensington paid him to drive these two men to Texas in a rented car. Austin police found the rental car and its driver. According to a police affidavit, police found the car's rental receipt, signed by the Arnold woman, in the glove box. Police also found drugs and another pistol hidden in the car.

The FBI arrested a Cleveland fugitive in her Arnold house. She was also accused of illegally possessing a handgun during a drug raid in 2001 at a house near Latrobe. The FBI also talked with her several times concerning a drug-related abduction of two women and a man along Fifth Avenue, New Kensington.

Numerous Valley residents have been arrested for selling drugs in central and southern Westmoreland County.

"We're seeing people from New Kensington show up in Derry and Latrobe," said Westmoreland County Detective Terry Kuhns, a former New Kensington police officer. "They move into rural areas because of lack of competition, and they can intimidate people by saying they're connected," Kuhns said. "Some people in rural areas just don't know any better."

Many other examples of Valley drug interests spreading their wings made headlines.

A drug dealer with Valley connections and almost a dozen others were prosecuted by the U.S. District Court in Wheeling, West Virginia.

In October 2001, a twenty-four year old man of New Kensington, pleaded guilty to selling cocaine. He received a sixteen-year prison term and fine for his role in the West Virginia case.

The New Kensington Police Department assisted the Ohio Valley Drug and Violent Crime Task Force that draws officers from federal and state law enforcement agencies and local police departments, according to U.S. Drug Enforcement Administration Special Agent Robert Manchis.

Valley officers also helped with the investigation of some of the others, from Cleveland and Pontiac, Michigan, who were convicted following the same grand jury investigation.

Westmoreland and Armstrong county prosecutors believe a failed drug robbery ended with a Kiski Township man being shot and beaten to death in the summer of 2001.

Three eighteen year old men, who were seventeen at the time of the killing, and three women were charged in the homicide of Larry Dunmire, forty-eight, of Sugar Hollow Road. The coroner said Dunmire died late June 14, 2001, or early the next day.

Prosecutors believe one of the women told the boys that Dunmire had drugs and money, and Dunmire was killed when he fought back. His body, hands tied with a nylon dog leash, was found along a road in Bell Township.

The pistol used to kill Dunmire, federal authorities said, was stolen from a Harmar gun dealer in February 2001.

"The expansion of drug dealers' territories is a result of suburban demand," said Ernest Batista, who directed the federal Drug Enforcement Agency office at Pittsburgh in the 1990s.

Dealers see a large number of suburban users driving into urban areas to buy drugs. "They begin to realize there is a market for it, and they go to rural areas," he said. "Cocaine networks exist. Most dealers are piggybacking Colombian heroin on the cocaine distribution routes," Batista added. The result of the cheaper, snortable Colombian heroin is a "bedroom community drug that is getting the all-American kids addicted."

"Heroin is rapidly pushing aside cocaine and other drugs as the major threat," said Victor Joseph, a Valley native who supervises the state attorney general's drug task force for the region.

"You'd be surprised. It's everywhere in the suburbs," he said, "and it's in your area."

Chapter 11

"Princes" of the City

G randpa received a letter from his mother back in Italy right after World War II. Her message stirred old feelings, "Your father is dying, but he keeps saying he wants to see his favorite son, Rocco, before he dies."

Her pleas touched his heart. His love for his mother had never subsided. Many times as a teenager, he had visited her secretly so "the Don" wouldn't know he was there.

But, his father knew.

From his dark world he watched, enviously and from a distance, jealous of the love of a mother and her son.

Now, love and hate and deep family ties tore at my grandfather's heart. How could he obey the summons of a father who had given him to another family to be raised? How could he rush to the side of someone who'd forced him to escape to America?

He decided to wait.

Finally he set aside six months to go back to his roots to pay last homage. A special audience was even set up so that he could meet with the Pope in the Vatican, something seldom arranged for Americanized Italians.

Upon his arrival in Italy my grandfather learned that he'd returned too late.

His father was dead.

Soon after that, his mother died too.

Grandpa stayed until his family's estate was settled. When he arrived back from Italy, he brought trunks full of trinkets, some of which I still treasure today. Included in it was an artwork that includes the Morelli family coat of arms and our family tree. The Morelli family roots sunk deep in the soil of Italy.

He left it to me.

During those years following World War II, the mob, the Morelli's and their adopted country prospered. The roaring 50s became an era of big money and big business for organized crime.

In the midst of this boom, I made my debut.

"It's a boy! Hugo had a prince!"

Word spread through New Kensington like wildfire.

Immediately, my black-sheep father was back in good graces. Hugo Morelli had sired a son. An heir.

He had married outside of the family, and had been shunned because of it. But now he had provided Rocco Morelli with a grandson.

All was forgiven. There was an heir. The family line would continue.

It was 1959, but the Morellis and their *compadi* had a communication network that superseded anything the FBI or local law enforcement possessed.

I do not exaggerate when I say that my birth was the cause of excitement and actually helped reinstate my father into the family. My father, whom I called "Pop," was the youngest of two sons and two daughters.

My grandfather was a *respingente*—a buffer between *la famiglia,* the Cosa Nostra and the people in the old neighborhood who needed favors or help with whatever it was that concerned them. He not only had favor with *la famiglia* in New Kensington, but was well-received in Pittsburgh and New York as well.

In those times, Italians were close because they lived near each other. Everyone knew everybody. There were no strangers in their midst. If you didn't have the right answer to *la famiglia* questions, you were asked to leave the same way you came.

Refusal could mean that you would always remember New Kensington or could never remember it again. Yes, people got killed.

Those loyal to the family never lacked for anything, even during the depths of the Great Depression. If anyone needed food, coal to heat their homes, or that precious commodity, gasoline, which was supposed to be rationed, my grandfather saw to it that their needs were provided.

For those with Mafia ties, no shortages of meat or sugar or nylons ever existed during World War II, either. However, my dad did not seem to appreciate all my grandfather provided.

Pop was tough and bullheaded. When he told his father that his high school football coach said he was talented enough to become a professional football player, my grandfather declared, "I'll break your legs for you if you continue to try to play such a ridiculous sport! It'll earn you no money and could get you crippled for life."

My dad's football career should have ended then and there. After all, his father had predicted it.

Indeed, my grandfather forbade him to participate in any high school sports at all.

My father defied him by playing tackle football in the streets with the rest of the tough guys in the neighborhood. But he made his father a prophet when he wound up with a busted knee, which ended any possibility of athletic fame.

Defying my grandfather was dangerous. But dad was *capotoste* — stubborn.

My dad joined the U.S. Army, just in time for the Korean War.

Perhaps it was my grandfather's influence or maybe it was my father's bad eyesight and bum knee, but while the rest of his outfit was sent into combat, my dad was transferred to a cushy stateside postmaster assignment. While they were shipped off to the confusing tragedy of the Korea Conflict, he was kept stateside in the southern United States.

"We really had it tough," my dad declared. "We ate the best, drank, and had a merry time with the Southern girls. My buddy and I even had our own Jeep to drive, so we would go swimming off of the base and frequently go to our favorite watering holes and brothels."

Italian guys from New York, New Jersey, Philadelphia and Pittsburgh found themselves stationed together and formed a close-knit Army family that nobody wanted to mess with. They stuck together all through their tour of duty.

To hear my father talk you would have thought there was more fighting and action where they were stationed stateside than overseas where the real war was being fought. In Korea, his battalion saw heavy action with most of his boot-camp buddies killed or severely wounded.

Throughout the years I have met a few of his Army buddies. According to Pop, they all wanted to fight for America, but didn't get a chance. My father came home from his tour of duty behind a desk.

But he hadn't gotten his rebellion against my grandfather out of his system. When he came home, he married a Russian-Ukrainian woman—a "Marushka"—against my grandfather's will.

My birth changed all that. Wisely my father gave me the name "Rocco" after my powerful grandfather, and all was forgiven.

No one mentioned my mother's background ever again. My dad's rebellion was over. A male child had been born to carry on the Morelli name.

Pop was a man of both action and words. He had a powerful presence. I'll never forget the time a Marine showed up uninvited to one of our wild high school parties at a friend's home. That Marine wanted to fight; it turned into an all-out brawl. The inside of that home was trashed.

I called Pop instead of the cops. Someone else phoned the police, but Pop arrived before they did. He stepped up to that Marine and punched him out cold.

When the Marine came to, the police had arrived and were already putting him into handcuffs. But what he wanted was to meet the first man who had ever knocked him out.

Dad was a peaceful, loving guy until you made him mad or tried to hurt someone he cared about. Once, a truck driver who was delivering supplies to our dry-cleaning shop came in with a chip on his shoulder and quickly picked a fight, hitting my dad's brother and knocking down my grandfather.

Pop smashed the guy into a cement wall.

In the alley outside, some thirty people began chanting, "Kill him, Hugo! Kill him!"

If Pop had realized that the man had hurt Grandpa Rocco, he might well have killed him right there in front of everybody.

The police even stood back and waited until Pop was finished pounding the man.

The truck driver was in pretty bad shape. Following a trip to the hospital, he was taken before a judge who had been a longtime friend of the family. He threw the book at the trucker.

My dad and all those present in the courtroom heard the big lug's plea, "Please, please, have mercy on me! I can't lose my job!" Sobbing, he added, "I've got a wife and kids to support."

My big-hearted Pop not only put up the money for the man's bail, but also made certain that the guy didn't have to do time. Then Pop influenced the company to keep him on their payroll.

I am told the driver had one more request of his own, "Please don't send me to New Kensington for any more deliveries."

I grew up in an empire of power that controlled everything from gambling to local politics. In the 1970s, during my teenage years, my grandfather was an influential man.

I was young and impressionable during the heyday of my family's "wise guys," men who wielded power and authority, and whose sons sought respectability by going into professions such as lawyers, judges, doctors and politicians at local, state and federal levels of government.

Those with musical talent even wrote and sang famous songs which represented the way we were and the way we lived in Little Chicago.

We were sure that the popular hit "The Candy Man" was written for one of the bosses who had been given that nickname.

No one thought anything of seeing Frank Sinatra or other famous Hollywood stars in New Kensington nightclubs. Many of the entertainers even privately attended the big bosses' funerals when they died, such as the infamous "Rat Pack" that was led by no other than "Old Blue-Eyes" himself.

My fondest memories are of my grandparents surrounded by the rest of our immediate family eating, drinking and enjoying good company around their dining room table. The Morelli family loved and respected each other and said they honored God as well as their fellow man.

People constantly came and went from my grandparents' house. My grandmother was forever cooking Italian feasts, which she prepared as a daily ritual. *"Manga, Manga,"* she would say, coaxing us to eat "some more."

My blessed mother, along with her mother Anna and my grandmother Maria all spoiled me with love and gifts and the very best of food. Today you would swear my mother was one hundred percent Italian.

Christmas Eve was like nothing else. You'd have thought that Grandma was cooking for an army. A week ahead, she started preparing for that one night of festivity.

An elegant woman, Grandma Maria was the "First Lady" of Little Chicago. All the women looked up to her. Dressed in the finest clothes that money could buy, she looked the same whether she was cooking or dining out.

I never saw her resembling anything less than a fashion plate. I'd have sworn she went to bed and got up that way. I believe Maria Morelli's life exemplified what a beautiful wife, mother, grandmother and great-grandmother could be.

Her death hit us all hard. My grandfather never recovered from it. They had spent sixty-three years together.

What a blessing they were to me.

Chapter 12

Leaving Little Chicago

"How did I leave the mob and live to tell about it?" Many have asked. It's simple.

I didn't. The mob left me. They left me alone because God the Father is bigger than any "godfather."

Most of us in the underworld believed in God, fearing Him with great respect. Without having the understanding and knowing the truth, though, we were lost in left field, hoping to one day hit a home run and make it to heaven.

On the other side of the coin, I was considered a stand-up guy in their eyes. I was respected because of my family and I didn't "snitch."

I was subpoenaed to go before the Grand Jury on organized crime in Pennsylvania. Well-rehearsed with our attorneys at our side, my partner Tony testified in my favor and changed his testimony to save the others from being indicted in the "Pizza Connection" investigation.

Tony was then rearrested for committing perjury. It was a much better alternative than getting "whacked."

I convinced the Boss to let Tony live. If push had come to shove, I would have defended Tony to my death.

After the hearings, Tony and I were driving back to New Kensington in my car. The Boss called on my car phone instructing me to call him when I reached my office.

The turning point had come. The verdict from the mob was about to be handed down from the "Boss" who would be our judge, jury, and possibly executioner.

Tony was still nervous and I was uncomfortable. My gut said it was O.K., but my mind was going a million miles a minute. I kept trying to recap our testimony and figure out if we had done our job of convincing the Grand Jury that there was no "Pizza Connection."

This was a matter of life and death. Not just for Tony, but for me as well.

I entered my office with Tony and made the call. The Boss instructed us, "Come to the restaurant."

As I hung up the phone, I took my automatic pistol out of my desk drawer. Seeing fear in Tony's eyes, I assured him everything would be all right. He knew I always "packed"; it was my insurance protection plan in those days.

In my mind I pictured the worst but hoped for the best. If all else failed, I planned to go out in style. I was prepared to take out the Boss and everyone who was present at the meeting.

I didn't know at the time that the Boss already knew the outcome of the hearings. He knew every word that was said to the Grand Jury, which was a closed session for security reasons.

How? They bought off a few of the grand-jurors.

Even if our testimonies had incriminated the rest of the mob, the jury's verdict could not indict unless it was unanimous. Tony and I were already charged, but without our testimonies against the others, they couldn't bring charges against the rest of the outfit.

Tony testified that his original accusations against all of us when he was busted were all fabricated in order to get himself off the hook. Tony took the fall.

Upon entering the back room of the restaurant, I noticed two strangers I never saw before sitting at the very back table observing every move Tony and I made. They were speaking in Italian very softly so we couldn't hear them. A few others came out of the kitchen and then the Boss.

We were welcomed with the customary family greeting—embracing and kissing each other on both cheeks. If a kiss on the lips had followed, it would have meant good-bye. We called it "the Kiss of Death." Instead we sat down and ate and drank as friends. The Boss assured us that we had done an excellent job by painting a cloud of doubt to the Grand Jury.

I wasn't surprised he knew. I understood corruption at all levels. He affirmed that he had a few "sticks" on the Grand Jury, even describing the one gentleman who called him immediately following the hearing.

He said now it would be up to us to beat the charges we each faced and assured us that it would all work out in the end. He said if we had to go to prison we would be taken care of. We could have money, cigars, and women, whatever we needed.

He wasn't joking about doing the time, but I never saw the money or women. The cigars I had to buy for myself.

Prison seemed like a good alternative to death by the dark chains of the "underworld." I was finally free, because "whom the Son sets free is free indeed."

Chapter 13

A Wise Man

From being a wise guy, I became a wise man of God. Who would have ever believed that the infamous Rocco Morelli, gangster, racketeer and womanizer would become addicted to the Bible?

I did!

After my conversion, my entire focus in life did an about-face. From serving the devil, I began to serve the Lord.

Family, friends, associates—all with whom I came into contact—knew something drastic had happened to me. I was not ashamed of the Gospel of Jesus Christ for I had learned from experience that it truly is the power of God unto salvation.

"You need to know Jesus," I kept saying to anyone who would listen. I think I literally scared the hell out of some of them.

Other times I know I came on so strong to friends of Pop and my grandfather that they decided the best thing to do was avoid me. I'm sure most of them shook their heads and said, "Young Rocco's gone off the deep end," but I hope at least they had to think about the change in me and what I said had caused it.

"Jesus" became my favorite word, but no longer taken in vain—the only way I had used His name for years.

In those days I thought I could improve the world by bringing them to the Lord, but I came to realize that God had to draw them to Him by way of His Holy Spirit.

God only uses us as a vessel.

I changed the "*My* Way" to "*His* Way" in my life. Once I submitted my life to Him, I found I could rely on Him more than myself or any other human being. God's way is the best way.

My life was never the same after I asked the Lord to take over. I truly believe that if it were not for my salvation and His saving grace, I would be dead and burning forever in hell by now.

Jesus delivered me from being a bitter man to being a better man with Him as my partner.

My return to court was scheduled. An hour before I was to appear before the judge and jury, the prosecution offered me a deal: "Plead guilty to all the charges, one-year probation and a fine."

I almost said yes, but inside of me the truth was yelling out, "No. No more lies. Face the judge and the public and tell the truth."

My answer? "No way!"

My attorney thought I was insane, but he did what I asked.

It was the longest week of my life. The charges were presented, play by play. I had been arrested a year earlier and managed to stay out of jail and plan my escape from justice.

Here it was finally my debut in court, I was Rocco Morelli, an untouchable who connived and schemed my way to the top of my world.

It didn't matter now. Somehow I knew it was all over. Everything I always wanted and worked for was no longer important. All that mattered to me now was that I finally found peace, the kind that passes all understanding.

I had asked the Holy Spirit to take control, claiming the Word of God in the book of Luke 12:11-12 that Jesus spoke:

"Now when they bring you to the synagogues and magistrates and authorities, do not worry about how or what you should answer, or what you should say. For the Holy Spirit will teach you in that very hour what you ought to say."

For the truth to be revealed, I knew I had to go to court.

My case had become quite complex. Multiple charges against me had resulted in two separate trials. The first trial didn't go well. The jury came back with the verdict "guilty as charged." The judge said he would continue my bond and delay sentencing pending a presentence investigation report.

Before my trial, my grandfather Rocco was stricken with a massive stroke. He had received an almost fatal blow to the head from an intruder that entered his home and robbed him. The man was African-American and a known thief. I was never a racist, but this made me hateful and prejudiced towards any black man. I wanted revenge on the creep who took a club to my grandfather's head with the intent to leave him for dead.

At age eighty-three, he somehow fought off the crazed animal. My grandfather threw his wallet at him begging for him to take his money, watch, anything in the house he wanted, pleading, "Just don't kill me!" The intruder finally quit and fled the scene.

Within minutes neighbors who had heard a disturbance came to my grandfather's aid. The police, ambulance and entire family were dispatched. I arrived just as the ambulance sped away. There was blood everywhere. An apparent struggle took place between my grandfather and his attacker. Things were scattered and broken in the house.

My dad and I talked to the police, who were our friends. My *compe* friend took charge of the manhunt. If the cops found him first, he might survive the night. Our hope was to find him before that and kill him like a mad dog.

The cops shook down everybody they could think of that would have known his whereabouts.

The irony is that no one found him, not the cops, not the family. It was as though he disappeared off the face of the earth. He got wind that he tried to whack the wrong old man. He knew he was a dead man walking on borrowed time.

My grandfather died after my sentencing, but never seemed to realize what had happened to me. His heart would have been broken if he had known.

No doubt, God's hand was upon me and He gave me favor. When it was time for my sentencing, the judge said, "I don't know why I am doing this, but I really believe you are a different young man. Different from about a year ago when you were first arrested." What could have been twenty years became only two.

The time came to say good-bye to my family. Racquel, just a toddler, looked up at me and I wondered, "How do you explain such a complicated mess to a child who is little more than a baby? How do you tell your own flesh and blood that her daddy is leaving?"

Torn apart inside, I swept her up into my arms briefly. What would become of Daddy's little girl? Sick to my stomach, I had to put her down.

Mom and Pop drove me to the courthouse where I turned myself over to the Sheriff. Both of them looked as if the gallows would be my next stop.

I was taken to the Westmoreland County Jail, a place where my role had been so different only a short time before, where I was the one wearing the badge. I was the one that brought the prisoners to be locked away into tiny cubicles with the door locked behind them.

This time I walked inside and the steel door clanged shut behind me. The sound of the key turning in the lock made me feel as if a vise were squeezing the life out of me.

One of the first inmates I saw had tattoos all over his body. He was a biker, just like the guy I vowed to get even with. All I could see was hate in his eyes, and I thought to myself, *Man, this guy might try to whack me.* All sorts of crazy thoughts and emotions ran through me as I was led to my new home.

For several long months I sat in Westmoreland County Jail and adjusted to life behind bars. I even got to know the biker. I found that underneath all his tough exterior, he was a man with feelings just like me.

No date was set for my departure to the state prison, so I tried to make the most of my relationships with the staff and other prisoners.

My heart soared when I found the former biker reading the Bible and praying to the Lord. His acceptance of Jesus as his Savior made my incarceration there of some value. In my heart I felt he was sincere and his commitment would save him from going back to his life-style of drugs and gangs.

The Lord gave Steve a burning desire to continue ministering to me and Steve became my mentor from outside the prison bars. When Steve would visit, he would read the Bible with me and encourage me as he fulfilled the verse, "I was in prison and you visited me."

"Why, Lord? Why do you want me in such a cold, dark place? What good can I do from here?" I would whisper after he left.

Such was my frequent prayer during the first days of my term. The answer came, not quite as dramatic as God's visit with Paul and Silas, but awesome to me.

There in the confines of my tiny cell, the presence of the Lord came upon me like the morning sun. In the stillness, He spoke to my heart: "Tell them about me. Share the testimony I have given you; preach my gospel to the captives and they will be set free!"

The Lord God Almighty was calling *me,* Rocco Morelli, chief among all sinners, to minister to the captives. It was so humbling.

I read the Word. *I prayed.* I sought His will. I read the verse: "I say to you, ask, and it will be given to you; seek, and you will find; knock, and it will be opened to you" (Luke 11:9).

I asked. *I sought.* I knocked.

And God opened many doors.

My job was to minister and share the Good News of Jesus Christ right there in prison. When I walked around smiling, the roughest, toughest guys on the block would look at me and growl, "What's your problem, man? You don't have any reason to be grinning. Don't you know you're just a jailbird?"

That gave me an opening to tell them, "Jesus has made all the difference in my life. He can in yours, too."

One by one, then by groups, the whole prison soon knew me as "the preacher."

Men behind cold steel bars can become stone cold hearted. Hard time turns them into skeptics. Most of them accused me of "acting" happy. The fact that I could smile didn't please them at all.

"You're just a fraud, man," one snarled at me. "Nobody could have anything to grin about in this hole. Best you wipe that smirk off your face before I wipe it off for you."

I wasn't acting. I had no control of the Holy Ghost. Jesus shined in me so that the love of Jesus shone through me. Many of them came to me, seeking answers to cure their own misery.

Over and over I had an opportunity to tell them, "Jesus loves you, too. He can do the same for you as He's done for me."

Before long, I had a full-time ministry within the walls of prison. God has no boundaries or limitations. Steve was my lifeline on the outside.

Steve came to visit and brought me new study books plus this message: "They want to know if you'll broadcast live from here."

"Broadcast live from here?" I was incredulous.

Then, I asked the obvious, "How can I do that while I'm in jail?" I couldn't imagine the warden letting TV crews and cameras into his domain.

Steve grinned, "No TV cameras will come in here. We won't do anything but get permission to put you on the phone and have the interview heard over our broadcast area. Just look at the good it'll do. Rocco, they want to do a mini testimony of what the Lord's doing behind bars. Everyone will want to listen because of who you are. There will be a great audience."

One thing that had to transpire was for me to get my pride out of the way. Enough bad publicity had already come to our family because of me.

"Lord," I prayed, "would me being on TV bring glory to your name? Having my voice reach the public from a jail cell can't be beneficial to you."

Thoughts of things Mom and Pop had said to me made me cringe. They told me that news of my arrest and conviction had gone nationwide. Headlines screamed "Mafia Member Jailed for Pushing Drugs" and "Public Official Convicted in Drug Connection."

One cousin even phoned my parents from Chicago and said he'd seen the reports there.

Sitting alone in my jail cell I had to sift out my feelings. My prayer became, "Somehow, Lord, take this cup from me."

Perhaps my situation of having to face the public from behind prison bars gave me some slight idea of how Jesus Himself must have felt when He went into the Garden of Gethsemane and knew what was ahead for Him.

Jesus wept when He returned three times only to find His disciples asleep. One whom He had loved so deeply would betray Him and He would have to face a humiliating, painful death on the Cross. The Lord Jesus knew what was about to take place. His Heavenly Father revealed how He would be treated to Him as He prayed alone in the garden.

There would be no mercy for the Son of the living God. Jesus knew His body would be subject to the sting of the whip and the agony of huge thorns pushed into His forehead. He knew He would be mocked and ridiculed for claiming to be the "King of the Jews."

I began to pray, pondering how Jesus had been betrayed and treated as the scum of the earth, of how the throngs cried, "Crucify Him!"

Shame swept over me. *He had done no crime.* He had not gone against the Father's will. He was without sin. In the short time I had come to know Him, I realized that all He'd suffered was to keep me from hell.

Me! I was chief among sinners.

I used and manipulated people for my advantage. In the end I, too, had been betrayed, but how could I possibly compare my life to that of my Savior? He had shed His blood, given His life for me so that I could have eternal life.

More than that, asking Him to forgive my sins and come into my heart had given me *new life* right here on earth.

Even in a prison uniform, I was free for the first time in my life. All the shackles of my past were gone. True love for my fellow man filled my heart.

I felt as if I'd been whitewashed inside and out. The scripture which says it best is, "Behold I make all things new."

All that stood in my way with the television broadcast was my pride.

I, Rocco Morelli, grandson and namesake of one of the founders of Little Chicago, had sinned. Even though I'd been set up for the crime that had jailed me, I had been guilty of so many other sins that I could hardly complain. *I belonged in jail.*

It bothered me, though, that thousands of people would turn on their TVs and hear me confess my crimes publicly.

I prayed and pondered the Lord's will, and I knew that sharing my conversion to the Lord Jesus was far more important than my pride. How fortunate I was in comparison to the Lord. Friends and family still stood by me.

When Steve came to visit again, I told him I felt the Lord nudging me to go ahead and do the TV broadcast. They would not see my face, but they would hear my voice and I could proclaim to viewers that giving your life to Jesus could and would change your life, regardless of your past.

My life was living proof.

That interview was a first, both for Cornerstone Television and the local prison system.

What a breakthrough. Such a humbling experience, too. I had to confess aloud things that I personally would have liked to have forgotten.

Months before, I had come to Jesus declaring I was a sinner, undeserving, not worthy of His love or mercy. Now I wanted to tell the world how He had reached out and touched my life, forgiving my past and filling me with such love for mankind. I wanted to share Him and His message.

It was incredible! God was using me from behind prison bars! *Our Heavenly Father does the impossible!* Those who had known me, or even known about me had to realize I was living proof.

Not everybody was won over, though. My wife was unconvinced. She didn't accept any of it. She didn't believe that I had changed.

She and my mom took over my office. One day a young, attractive woman came by and asked for me. Among the hidden sins of my past was a secret affair with this woman. I'd broken off my relationship with her after giving my life to Jesus. Yet, my spouse sensed something. Her woman's intuition kicked in. On her next visit to the jail, she looked me in the eye and demanded to know.

"Tell me there wasn't anything between you and this woman?" she asked.

I wanted so much to tell her it had been nothing. I could have lied. I was a great liar.

Things had changed now and I couldn't lie, even to spare my wife terrible pain. The pre-Jesus Rocco would have lied straight-faced, without any shame to my game, but Jesus wiped out all the lies.

Shamefaced, I told her the truth. In all my years I have never seen such hurt in a pair of eyes. I begged her to forgive me, to understand that such things were in the past.

She did not believe any of my words. I lost her trust. She went home without anything resolved about my past affair. I wanted to convince her that I had changed and assure her that she could trust me. She never visited me again.

Prisoners were allowed a few phone calls on certain days. Whenever I had the opportunity, I would plead with her on the phone.

One evening I kept talking, coaxing, begging and cajoling her to forgive me. She was cold and unresponsive. She told me in a flat voice that she was filing for divorce.

"What about the baby?" I said. "What about Racquel?"

She didn't answer.

One day as I tried to persuade her, a huge inmate behind me in line was waiting less and less patiently for me to turn over the phone.

My conversation with my wife was so critical to me that I ignored his gestures. But he wanted his turn, and he got more and more ugly about it.

Finally, frustrated at what she was saying, and disgusted with him for pressuring me, I threw down the receiver.

"It's yours!" I yelled at him in a show of my old Italian temper. I was immediately remorseful. I knew no one would see Jesus in me acting like that.

Letting out a growl, the inmate started after me wielding a sharpened pencil in hand, which he intended using as a 'shank' to take me out.

Cursing, he yelled, "I'm going to kill you, m____ f____."

I turned around to face him putting out my hands as if to welcome a fight.

"Come on!" I yelled with gusto.

That brought the whole jail's attention. Everyone jumped up, including the guards, to watch what was going to happen next.

I was flushed with shame.

God spoke to my heart and told me to walk away. I trembled, because that was impossible. I had never in my life backed away from a fight.

I heard myself saying, "I'm going back to my cell to read my Bible."

Impossible. What a change.

I thought of all the times I'd egged on a fight. I'd jump into battle just to lend a hand, sometimes to help a total stranger, but mostly just for the fun of a scrap. I had jumped into lots of fights wearing my policeman's uniform. All too many times when I'd tear into some guy beating up on a woman, the damsel-in-distress would leap on me, screaming, "Don't you hurt my husband!"

As I retreated to my cell that day, all eyes were on me. Even the guards gawked in disbelief, especially when the big lug stopped dead in his tracks. They said it was as though he ran into an invisible wall and saw a ghost. He froze and turned around as though it never happened. I believe he was met by a wall of angels that the Lord sent to protect me.

My backing down amazed me more than anybody. I kept moving toward my cell and didn't look back. If they wanted to think of me as a coward, that was how it had to be. I knew God had spoken to me and it would ruin my witness if I had engaged in a free-for-all.

Time went on, and I thought my wife might be softening her attitude toward me. I received a few letters and notes from her, but one day a guard took me into an office to serve divorce papers. I felt as if I'd been stabbed.

Back in my cell, I sank to my knees. I prayed. I wept. I screamed from frustration and despair. "Lord," I wailed, "I don't want to lose my family!"

It was my prayer, but I also knew that "what you sow you also reap." I'd sown mistrust and my wife had just cause for her decision. Even in God's eyes, I knew she had just cause for her wrath.

Infidelity is the only real reason for divorce listed in the Bible. Nothing else could have hurt her or our little girl more than my unfaithfulness.

My wife had made her decision, and I was in no position to dispute it. Being an inmate makes it difficult to fight things taking place on the outside. How I would have loved to have had the Lord "take this cup from me," even though I knew I had no right to expect it.

After much prayer, I realized I needed to focus on working in the prison ministry. There was little I could do about saving my marriage from behind bars except pray that my wife would forgive me.

Remember that huge dude who'd demanded the telephone? You'd think he'd have considered me a pansy because I refused to fight.

That wasn't the case at all. He began to watch me and then, unexpectedly, appeared at Bible study.

His decision to accept Christ was startling, for he was of the Muslim Faith, but his seriousness about knowing Jesus on a more intimate basis was even more awesome.

When we talked about the Holy Spirit and the gift of speaking in tongues, he declared, "I want to do that. If it makes you feel closer to the Lord, I need to know how."

This huge guy, who I called "Bubba," listened intently whenever anyone spoke in tongues. "How you do that, man?" he demanded. "I want to talk like that, too."

"Just ask the Lord to give you your prayer language," I encouraged him over and over.

He had a tremendous singing voice and we usually heard his praises in song whenever he was in the shower.

One day the bathroom door burst open and he came out shouting.

"I got it! I got it!" he shouted.

It was hard not to burst out laughing, because in all his excitement, he'd forgotten that he was still dressed only in what he'd worn into the shower. Shouting in tongues, he danced around the room, delighted and completely oblivious that he was stark naked.

The Lord constantly provided our needs. Often He did it through friends on the outside, especially Steve Totin, who seemed to have divine direction as far as all the new prison converts' needs.

There was no doubt in my mind that he was led by the Holy Spirit, because my spiritual mentor always seemed to show up when my morale had reached its lowest. He brought books and enthusiasm and shared the Word with the other inmates and me.

I spent much of my time with Jesus, often because there was no human with which to share.

My parents came to visit as often as they were allowed, but they couldn't always be there for me.

I had to lean on the Lord.

Chapter 14

The Big House

"Get your gear. You're moving out!" For a moment I couldn't even focus my thoughts. Where was I? Awakened from a deep sleep, I looked at the clock, then out the window. Dawn hadn't even arrived. What was going on? Suddenly it hit me. It's December 4—my birthday. Maybe they were letting me go home.

"Are you giving me a birthday present? Are you going to let me out of here?" I asked. Maybe, just maybe, they were going to let me out on good behavior since I'd already served six months of my sentence. The guard grumbled, "Not unless you think that going to Western Pen is a present."

Western Pennsylvania State Penitentiary was known to both the law and the underground as the "The Wall." They were moving me out in the middle of the night so that no one, including my father and *la famiglia*, would know what they were doing.

Two men herded me outside and into a squad car. The loading dock was bleak and dark. The cold winter wind cut through to the marrow of my bones. The chill outside was no worse than the one shaking my inner being.

How could this be happening to me? Western Pen was where only hardened criminals were incarcerated. All through the lengthy ride I prayed, "Lord, go with me."

I memorized many scriptures concerning Paul's imprisonment. They paraded through my mind along with many of the Psalms concerning deliverance from evil.

Every other time, I'd been in the driver's seat. This time I was the back seat passenger with no choice as to where I was going and what was taking place.

At the Pen I was given a drab prison uniform, I was led to a cell after my chauffeurs filled out the necessary papers. I can't honestly say that as I sat in a dismal penitentiary cell for the first time that I didn't consider all the possibilities of what I could have done.

Sitting there alone, looking at all the other men who had been convicted of major crimes, I sought some solace from God. "Lord, help me." And He did.

During the first few weeks, my spirits were lifted whenever I got out my Bible and spent time with my Heavenly Father.

Mom and Pop came to visit whenever they could. Ashamed to tell my daughter that her daddy was in prison, I thought my heart would break open when they told her that "Daddy's in school."

No one could stand to tell her the truth, and in a way, I guess I was in school—the ultimate school of hard knocks.

Steve made visits to Western Pen just as he had to the Westmoreland County Jail. In a short time, I'd adjusted to the fact that I had eighteen months to spend in this facility for hard-core criminals.

I could tell by Pop's demeanor that my incarceration was eating him up. The fact that the law had moved me to Western Pen irked him. Angry that I'd been set up and furious that I'd been convicted, Pop held the cops, lawyers, judges, and anyone else who had been a part of my arrest and conviction responsible.

His only son did not belong in such a prison.

Even though he wanted to go after them with a vengeance, Mom and I tried to convince him that such a move would be futile. It might even get me into additional trouble, I told him.

One night in the midnight hour, I felt I must have been awakened by an angel. I had a vision which I knew came directly from the Lord. I envisioned my father orchestrating acts of retaliation for what had happened to me.

I knew the time, the place, and the people he intended to get back at. Heartsick, I even knew whom he planned to use to accomplish the task. Pop's plan was for a bloody massacre, starting with the "snitch," then the arresting officers and the judge.

I knew the Lord was showing me all the details so that I would stop Pop. He needed to read the scripture: "Vengeance is mine, saith the Lord."

The next day Steve arrived at the prison. I could tell from his demeanor, that he, too, had a burden he was carrying. Within a few minutes I heard from my spiritual mentor's lips the same revelation from God that I experienced the night before. Steve also had been shown what Pop was planning to do.

Mom's longtime prayer partner was the next to share with Mom how the Lord laid on her heart the retaliation plan that Pop had become determined to put into action.

When my father came to visit, I had no choice but to confront him about his plans. With his eyes wide open in disbelief, I spelled out exactly who, what, where, and why he planned to act out his vengeance.

"How could you know all that?" Pop asked in amazement.

"The Lord showed me," I replied.

My father stood transfixed in astonishment as I revealed that God also showed Steve and Mom's friend the same thing.

My father was so awestruck that he decided he'd better forget his retaliation plans. Instead, he rededicated his life to Jesus.

I made up my mind when I went to jail that I'd make the most of my time behind bars doing whatever I could for Jesus.

I was filled with a deep concern for my fellow prisoners. They often sought me out to talk about seemingly impossible problems, such as family situations, and I would pray for them.

Many of them came from dysfunctional homes. I became more and more aware of how much my own parents had tried so hard to give me a normal life.

You may find this difficult to understand. How could I think I had a normal family? They were associated with the mob. My dad knew hitmen and he considered some of them good friends.

How could this be normal? It was part of the generational curse. Over the years, my family just accepted evil as part of doing business. You may have heard of cultures where truth need not be told to an enemy, and a gifted liar is considered an asset to the community. In some societies a thief, such as Robin Hood, Aladdin, or Jesse James, is admired.

What about a culture that accepts adultery? Ever been to France? Or prostitution? Look at Holland. What about a culture where murderers are heroes? Just look at America. Hollywood glamorizes mobsters like Billy the Kid, Bonnie and Clyde, and Al Capone.

Much of our motion picture industry praises evil as good and mocks those things which are good, making them look ridiculously stupid.

So, how can anybody be critical of my family? We believed in loyalty, respect to our elders and death before dishonor.

You may wonder why this book doesn't go into detail about crimes committed by family. The answer is that I am no snitch. I am responsible for my sins. It is up to me to seek forgiveness and make retribution if I have hurt anyone. I am not responsible for the sins of others. *Neither are you.*

Despite some rather glaring flaws, my imperfect family gave me deep and unquestioning love. They nurtured me through good times and bad. On her knees, my wonderful mother prayed me through my childhood, my wild teens, and my wise guy young adulthood. She stood with me whether I was being an angel or a rebel.

In jail, I met men who'd never known their fathers, and whose promiscuous mothers had only a list of suspects and a constant parade of boyfriends who stayed for a few days or a few years.

All my life, I'd known nothing but close family ties, heritage and unquestionable love. In jail, I found myself ministering to guys who'd been abused in terrible ways.

Jail gave me time to consider my past misadventures. Solitude was mine. I had endless hours to just sit on my bunk and ponder how I'd fouled up my life so much.

Nothing bad that happened was my parents' fault. Many times I had, as a teenager, impatiently endured my parents' lectures. Many times they told me what I should or shouldn't do. Many times I deliberately went out and disobeyed them.

I tried Pop's patience over and over again.

The lives of other inmates made me aware of how great my own family was. Often my fellow inmates told me of growing up in the streets with no supervision. They claimed that most of the time nobody cared where they were or what they were doing as long as they stayed out of people's hair at home.

Many of them had come from single-parent homes and their mothers had to work outside the home long hours to make enough to feed, clothe and house them. Some had no parents at all, just grandmothers who tried to do their best.

Accepting the love of their Heavenly Father was not easy for these guys. A father's love was not something they could comprehend. They were abandoned by their earthly dads.

Convincing them about the sacrifice of God's Son for their sake was even more difficult. Once they began to accept the meaning of love, they began to see how their Creator could care so much for them.

Convincing them further that Jesus bled and died for them out of His great love for them, even though they had committed incredible sins against God, was not simple. Once they accepted the depth of His sacrifice, they became willing to give their hearts to Him and to ask Him to forgive them and become Lord of their lives.

What a difference Jesus made in them. My fellow inmates' language, attitudes and their entire being changed once they accepted Jesus as Lord.

Convicted burglars, rapists and con-men searched the Word and attended Bible studies. Admitted muggers and drug dealers looked forward to prayer meetings. Their change was as obvious as mine. Part of my growth during my jail term came about because of Steve's faithfulness in keeping in touch. Both he and Doc Iozzi accepted collect calls anytime I needed to have someone pray with me.

Something I noticed missing in my life was that smug cockiness that I'd had for so long. The Great Rocco that I'd envisioned became just another jailbird—how *humbling!*

When things got too hectic in prison I had no one to turn to but Jesus. By hectic, I mean sometimes things were horrible. Regardless of the guards' watchful eyes inmates continued to get into scraps.

When tension grew between a couple of prisoners, it wasn't unusual to see them sparring in a corner, pounding flesh and drawing blood.

Sexual and physical abuse happened any time the guards' eyes shifted. Leaders would enlist gang members to fight other gangs for them. One lifer confessed to me that he'd had all he could stand of prison existence and he wanted to do himself in.

"You mean suicide?" I asked him.

"I wish they would have killed me before they sent me to this hole. You can't call this existence, and I don't have a chance for parole. This is a slow, dying death. I'm gonna kill myself the first chance I get."

I told him there is hope in Jesus, but he wouldn't listen. He said, "I did wrong and I need to pay for my sins."

Sirens blared one night. Voices came down the line through the cells and my heart sank. *I knew.*

My lifer had made good his threat. He hung himself in his cell with his belt. That night I prayed that I could be released from my punishment soon.

To top it off, I learned that the man who attacked my grandfather was on his way to prison. I got word that he had been shot in Ohio and now was extradited back to Pennsylvania. I was informed of his whereabouts and presented with the opportunity to have him killed for his crime against my grandfather.

A big part of me said "yes" to the proposition of sweet revenge. But the other, growing part of me heard a still voice say, "Vengeance is mine, says the Lord." (Romans 12:19) Therefore I knew God's way was better than mine. I learned in the Scriptures that I also had to forgive him, but it wasn't easy.

I prayed for God to save him and for the Lord to forgive me of my hatred that had made me an angry, bitter man. The burden was lifted and the peace of God that passes all understanding was mine.

Soon after that, I was transferred to Greensburg State Correctional Institution, a mid-range security prison, to finish my time. One of the staff there who made my existence endurable was the chaplain. And of all things, our spiritual advisor in prison was a *woman!*

Dorothy had compassion, but determination and wisdom, too. While I was doing my time, we became friends. When she declared, "Rocco, I've heard a lot of people confess Christ as their Savior while they're here, but when they get out, they forget Him right away. I don't think you're going to be one of them."

Her faith in me gave me more faith in myself and my ability to walk with the Lord once I was on the other side of the prison walls.

One time when she had a physical problem, she came to our Bible study for prayer. Dorothy was one of our stabilizing factors when everything around us was chaos. With her help and the support of other Christian inmates, I prayed that we could all make it through without anything disastrous happening to any of us.

Chapter 15

My "Coming Home Party"

S ometimes it seemed as if I would spend eternity in that bleak place. I had to keep my eyes on Jesus so that I wouldn't sink into the mire.

The other thing I did was keep my eyes on the calendar, anticipating the day when I would be able to go before the parole board.

My sentence was for two years, yet I had the possibility of parole in fifteen months.

When my long-awaited "D" (for *Determination*) Day arrived, I prayed for favor that I might get out of my punishment and somehow get back to a "normal" existence.

The parole board members scrutinized me as I walked into the room.

They fired questions at me.

"Do you have a work place?"

"A home?"

God bless my parents. Pop had promised that I could work at his dry-cleaning establishment and Mom readied my room back at home.

"Do you think you're rehabilitated?"

I had a well-thought-out answer: "Yes, I feel that I have been. I've given my life to Jesus, and I hope to be of value to Him when I get out of here."

I'm certain they'd heard such expressions of faith and loyalty to Jesus before. The pledges were far too often mere scams by inmates champing at the bit to get out of jail.

I'm also certain that parole board members had seen the "converts" return far too soon. The difference between most of them and me was my behavior in jail and the words of Dorothy, the chaplain, who went to bat for me. I was talking the talk, but also walking the walk.

They decided I could go home nine months early. I thanked the Lord and them.

My next "D" (for deliverance) day was about to happen. Mom and Pop and Racquel were waiting as I walked outside the prison. *Free!* No one who hasn't spent time within the confines of a cell can appreciate the feeling of freedom.

I was tempted to kiss the ground.

Instead I kissed the three who had come to bring me home. Pop insisted, "You tell us where you want to go, son. Anywhere you want, we're game."

It might have been nutty, but I wanted to be near people. "People!" I told him. "I want to go where people are. Let's go to the shopping mall."

Mom laughed. "What do you want to eat?" she asked.

Racquel was sitting in my lap. "Where would you like to go, honey?" I asked her. Without hesitation my four-year old announced the name of her favorite seafood restaurant, Red Lobster.

With a grin, I realized at four she already had a mind of her own. "That it is!" I declared, "I'm buying. I saved $200 for work I did in there, and I want to treat you."

Racquel looked up at me. Big-eyed, she asked, "Daddy, are you ever going back to that school?"

Hugging her, I spoke words that I meant with all of my heart, "No, baby. Daddy is *never* going to do anything that will make me ever go back to that school. I promise."

In my heart a prayer was formed during that coming-home party:

"Lord, don't ever let me get involved with evil again. Deliver me from evil!"

That was and remains my fervent request.

Chapter 16

Outside Prison Walls

Every day I read the Bible and prayed that the Lord would direct my path and keep it straight. Sin was something I wanted to put behind me, as far as the north is from the south.

The courts had put a man in charge of seeing to it that I walked my talk.

Jim California, my parole officer, came snooping around at any time he wished to check up on me at my job at the cleaners. Sometimes he spent quality time just giving encouragement to his former jailbird client. This bothered me at first, but I realized in a short while that he was working to get me established as a rehabilitated man. He was my friend, not my enemy.

In a month's time he agreed to let me go back and work at my former office, where I was still qualified to be a notary public. Clients came to get papers notarized and welcomed me back.

Life was looking up. However, not everyone believed I had changed. Many were still betting that I would return to organized crime. I was tested, even by the arresting cops. They even convinced the state to revoke my notary license. My mom took over the business and eventually sold it. Somebody even had the guts to shoot at my office. I guess they wanted to see how I would respond. It was by God's miraculous grace that I no longer would give in to the devil's traps.

I missed not having a wife.

One day, I visited Doc Iozzi's office. A real knockout smiled her interest in me, and I succumbed. She was filled with ambition and had great plans for her future. Doc Iozzi had been involved in nutritional products and through another friend I learned of a network opportunity in multilevel sales. The woman in his office became enthusiastic along with me about selling nutritional supplements.

At the same time, I started with another company, selling air filtration systems. Before long, I popped the question to her. She said yes, and Steve found us a minister to perform the ceremony.

Without consulting King Jesus, we decided to set off for Erie, Pennsylvania, to begin a new career where Mom and Pop lent me a sizable sum so I could have a fresh start. The setup was ideal, except I was trying to run on Rocco power instead of relying on Jesus.

Since we'd decided to go full-tilt into the multilevel sales networking business world and make tons of money we went out and socialized every night.

We drank with our clients.

Was this what I should be doing? I rationalized that it was the only way to make it in the world. Why would the Lord care if I had a scotch-on-the-rocks anyway? We were attending wonderful services at the Assembly of God Church, so what would a few drinks hurt? Plus, we were tithing our income, which was sizable. That eased my conscience. I guess I thought I was buying my way out of trouble.

It's impossible to hide your life-style from God, and we soon learned it wasn't possible to hide it from our Christian brothers and sisters.

Steve and my friends at Cornerstone got wind of what I was doing. They asked me to explain.

Didn't I know what kind of witness I was making? We ran into every kind of difficulty. Money was not so much the problem, but other things and other people caused us to have serious arguments and our life-style was getting out of control.

Eventually we separated, and then divorced.

Mom and Pop had tried to encourage me to do right while I lived in Erie, but I'm sure they sensed I had stepped out of bounds. I was doing things that neither my Heavenly Father nor my earthly Father wanted for me. I was going to church, but I wasn't living a God-honoring life.

Like an errant child, my world came crashing down around me as my second marriage fell apart.

For one year I rebelled and tried to run from God.

That year of my life was hell on earth for me. I learned what the Bible meant when it said, "No one who puts his hand to the plow and turns back is fit for the kingdom of God."

I had offered my life to Jesus, but turned my back on Him. I let the devil take over in many aspects of my living.

Chapter 17

The Prodigal Returns

When the legalities of my divorce were finalized I knew what had been wrong. I'd gone back into the world. I had left behind the source that had made me free. Miserable, I knew I had to repent. Falling to my knees, I wept. "Lord," I cried, "Forgive me."

I made certain that I obeyed man's laws. I was determined not to serve time ever again. But I ignored God's laws. My prayer that day was, "Lord, I give up. I'm miserable. I'll go where you want me, and I promise that I will follow Your will from now on."

I came to know and listen to the Holy Spirit while I was in jail, but I drifted away from His guidance. What a mess I made of my life when I ignored His influence.

I felt very strongly that I needed to break all the bondages of my illicit past.

I heard that they were having deliverance services at a church in Pittsburgh. One night in 1994 I found the Holy Spirit leading me that direction. Rev. Gary Mitrik prayed over me. I fell to the ground again, and my Savior delivered me.

My lust left. I walked out of that church knowing that good had triumphed over evil. The prince of darkness could no longer control me.

Jesus was waiting with open arms. I asked Him to forgive me once more. I offered Him my life and He willingly accepted. Once I recommitted myself to the Lord and begged His forgiveness for falling away from His will for my life, I knew I dared not turn away from the calling He had on my life again, and I knew in my heart that I never wanted to be out of His favor again.

I started studying the Bible again, feeding my spirit. I kept asking the Lord where He wanted me to go and what He wanted me to accomplish. After much prayer, I knew that I was to return home to New Kensington and start a prison and evangelism outreach ministry.

My carnal mind began weighing such a move. How would the folks in my hometown react to my starting a ministry there?

Would anyone there ever be able to think of me as anything but a mobster or a crooked cop from Little Chicago? How was I ever going to convince anyone that I'd lost my conceit and my swagger? How would I prove to them that Jesus had become the only Source I had?

One more thing concerned me. "Lord," I prayed, "how are my parents going to feel?"

When I told them, they where supportive. Mom and Pop opened their hearts and their home to me. They had no fatted calf to kill, but my mother cooked me feast after feast. Whatever I said I wanted, she seemed to delight in fixing it for me.

My personal finances had dwindled to almost nothing. During the four years that I'd lived in Erie during my second marriage and divorce, I'd spent considerable money trying to act out the role of a successful multilevel sales big shot. In the end, the thing I hated most was the fact that I'd put some of my parents' money in jeopardy too.

The problems that Pop had over the years with his knees had not improved with time. Movement became painful, and I knew he was looking forward to the day when he could retire and not have to stand on his feet all day at the dry cleaning plant.

One of the things that kept him from attaining that goal was his son. My father and mother had loaned me a substantial sum to buy the house and office in Erie. When I came home, they could have spent their time reminding me of their needs and sacrifices, but never did. Still, that obligation weighed heavily on my conscience.

Mom and I talked often. We prayed about my future. I couldn't help but think of how much of her life she had spent asking the Lord to guide her son in the right direction.

Opportunities opened up for me to go into prisons and jails and share what the Lord had done for me.

I had not only walked in the inmates' shoes, but I had felt the loneliness, the humility, and the frustration of being confined like an animal behind bars. Prison was as close to hell as I ever want to be.

Because of being able to share a similar experience as each of them, prisoners all listened intently as I told them how knowing Jesus had set me free, even when I was physically restrained like them.

Chapter 18

Help Cometh

I put all my first efforts into street witnessing and small revivals. Since music had always been my *forte*, I had little difficulty getting Christian musicians interested in forming a band. Their magnificent praise and worship touched hearts. At evangelistic meetings, after much prayer, I found the Holy Spirit beginning to speak through me.

Imagine my joy and surprise to find my sermons were truly anointed.

After one of the meetings a beautiful black woman came to me and said she felt led of the Lord to pray for and minister with me. Teralyn became my soul sister in Christ, encouraging and even at times correcting me so that my talk and walk for God would be more effective.

Phone calls began to come in from all across western Pennsylvania. At one meeting, a man came up to me after the crowd dispersed and said, "I'm Earl Fingerman. I am a born-again believer."

He shared his testimony with me and I realized that the Lord breaks all the bondages of each of our pasts in a different way. Earl is Jewish and is proud that he is among God's chosen people. He even takes greater pride in the fact that he came to know Jesus whom he refers to as "Yeshua" (Hebrew for "Jesus") as his personal Savior.

Earl's story is different from mine. He'd been successful, but through a series of events, he became poverty stricken. In his need, he traveled across the country and wound up at a stranger's home where he met Jesus.

Since that time his life has turned around.

Earl proudly professes Jesus as his Lord. When he came up to chat with me, I knew the Holy Spirit had touched him. How thrilling it was for him to say, "I believe the Lord wants me to help you with your ministry."

At that point I had no notion of how much interest Earl had, but his enthusiasm and support in the months that followed caused me to nickname him my "Joshua." Moses depended on Joshua to do battle for him. I learned to depend on Earl.

We tried several plans to get the ministry out of the beginning stages, but nothing seemed to work except small revivals, street witnessing and one-on-one with prisoners and individuals.

Earl even had a mailing made up and sent out to 750 churches. He declared, "If we only get one percent, I'll be happy." One reply came, and that lone church canceled before we ever got to minister there.

My Joshua was downhearted.

Somehow the Lord kept me from becoming depressed. Somehow, I knew that if we didn't push and try in the flesh that the Lord would answer our needs.

Doing a personal inventory, I could see that a lot of things were amiss in my life. I needed sufficient finances to go off on my own.

I wanted a Godly, loving wife, one who would travel with me and be an asset to the ministry.

I could have let these facets weigh me down so that I couldn't function, but *I knew* that if I was obedient to the Lord, He would provide everything in His time.

I had to wait as it says in Isaiah to get my wings like the eagles, to not grow weary or faint. This scripture became very real to me.

I have learned to entrust everything in my life to God and wait for my wings so I could fly.

Chapter 19

Great Changes

One afternoon, while I was chatting on the phone, another call interrupted the conversation. The caller was a Salvation Army officer offering his facility to hold services for the community.

After that, events took place that changed my world in a matter of a few months. One of my concerns had always been for my daughter. I felt as if my misdeeds had taken her away from me; now we had time together.

My Racquel was becoming a young woman. I began to witness and tell her about the Lord. I wanted her to know that Jesus loved me enough to forgive me.

My prayer was that she could come to forgive me too. Racquel only heard bits and pieces detailing my past, mostly half-truths from her mother and others that distorted what really happened. I was wrong for what I did—I admitted being an ex-convict and criminal. One thing I was not, however, was a bad father. I purposed in my heart to let my daughter know I loved her and that none of my actions were her fault. Racquel tried to believe me and struggled with the rumors that I was a no good so-and-so and a deadbeat dad. I figured my actions would speak louder than words and continued to love her and fight to see her as often as possible. Racquel grew up missing me and wanted a relationship with her dad, not step dads or other men. I fought for custody and failed. Looking back at the circumstances I never had a fair chance to be the dad I wanted to be and the father she needed through the most important times of her life. We both agree today that the system failed us but God has restored us. We are making up for lost time with the help of the Lord who reconciled us to Him and each other.

It all began at that time. My beautiful little girl accepted Jesus into her heart and said she forgave me. Even greater joy came when she was baptized in the Holy Spirit. Such a blessing came as I watched her grow up spiritually as well as physically. My concern about my daughter had been resolved through prayer and the Lord's guidance.

Another major concern still existed. I truly wanted a mate, but the only way I'd even consider taking out a girl was if I felt a definite leading from the Lord.

Mom and I talked about it at great length. She assured me she recognized the need in my life and she'd been in prayer for me to find the right person.

There'd been many single females wherever I spoke, but none of them ever quickened my spirit. If Jesus wanted me to meet a mate, I was certain He would let me know that He had arranged it.

One night I was going to a Full Gospel Business Men's meeting to speak in a tiny burg in the mountainous area of Pennsylvania. On the way the Lord spoke to me, "You are going to meet your wife tonight."

Upon entering the meeting hall one of the hosts informed me, "There are three nice single girls here tonight."

Glancing around I spied one who smiled at me. Her face was filled with the love of Jesus. "Lord," I asked, "is she the one?"

Determined to divert my mind from my personal concern, I prayed that my words would be of great value to those who'd come to listen.

"Lord, use me," I prayed. I managed to put my personal thoughts aside until the altar call. Then I put a fleece out, "Dear Jesus, if she's the one, have her be first in line for prayer."

Upon opening my eyes, there she stood! Again she flashed her smile that said "Jesus." Not flirtatious, only loving and kind. That very night Christine invaded my heart and I knew that she was the one that the Lord had chosen for me.

After the meeting I approached her and she invited me to go to Perkins Restaurant for fellowship with everyone. As we were sitting there the Lord spoke to her dad, "This is your new son-in-law."

I asked Christine if she would like to go out the next day, as I was staying at one of my Christian brother's home for the night. She accepted. But I wanted her dad's approval. So I took the old-fashioned approach and asked her father if it was O.K. to take his daughter out.

His reply was "Who am I to stand in the way of the Lord?"

I thought to myself, "He must know something, too."

I arrived at Christine's house after church. She greeted me with a warm smile. We had a great day, going to Kinzu Bridge, trail walking the hills, eating ice cream, laughing, and sharing in the Lord.

Christine told me she had been praying to God for a Holy Spirit-filled, obedient man of God to enter her life. She went through a divorce and had a lot of hurts. But through it all she grew stronger and closer to the Lord. The Lord had been preparing Christine.

When she visited my parents' home the next weekend, Mom and Pop's approval was most evident.

Racquel's response to Christine became my major concern. My daughter tickled me with her admission, "I'm praying for you to get a good Christian wife." Knowing that, I prayed after meeting Christine that my daughter would not be jealous, but would like my choice and share my joy.

I prayed that her approval would confirm that the Lord had chosen her to be my wife and Racquel's new step-mom.

Any apprehension I had disappeared after the two of them had been together a short time. They truly liked each other. Hallelujah!

Christine and I became better acquainted. She told me that she'd always yearned to travel; something I felt was a necessity for anyone who wanted to share my life and ministry. She was an accountant, something that could be invaluable for us in the future.

A few months later I was at Christine's home. I knew the Lord had revealed to her that I was to be her husband. As we were talking we both agreed that we "would become one."

We wondered when we should wed. We both agreed to write down on separate sheets of paper the date we both felt in our hearts.

When we shared what we had written, we both laughed and hugged each other. Both of us had written Christmas Eve.

Three months later we were joined together. It was Christmas Eve.

Anyone reading this book from start to finish might be astonished at what the Lord can do. It is nothing short of miraculous that He could transform a hot-headed, self-indulgent Mafia kid to a man who has dedicated his life to helping others find the Lord Jesus as their personal Savior.

In writing this, neither my wife nor I know what is in store for us.

But who does?

Nothing is ever really settled except that Jesus is the Alpha and Omega, the beginning and the end. Christine and I will serve Him the rest of our lives wherever He leads us.

As I've reflected on the past when I was in the mob and could have been killed, I realized that the Lord has always had His hand on me, and His angels must have been assigned to protect me because He has a job for me to do. He has a plan and purpose for everyone who will follow Him. My prayers often ask Him for guidance and direction and for wisdom and knowledge to do it well.

He can do the same for you.

The New Man & Ministry

R occo Morelli Ministries International is an evangelistic and prison ministry, operating as an interdenominational nonprofit Christian organization that ministers the good news of Jesus Christ to prisoners, at-risk kids and the lost around the world.

Today I am an ordained minister serving as an Evangelist and International Speaker. We are also network members of the Coalition of Prison Evangelists.

The Lord has taken me to England, Ethiopia, Africa, Scotland, Turks and Caicos Islands and various places throughout the United States to minister and share my testimony. Our goal is to teach, disciple and raise up godly individuals for the family of Christ.

We are focused on reaching prisoners, ex-offenders, victims, their families and the community. We want to be the Holy Spirit's instruments in regenerating ex-offenders and prisoners and reintegrating families, both socially and spiritually, by ministering to the whole person through spiritual care programs.

Prisoners' marriages can be saved and restored to wholeness in Christ. Children of inmates can be brought into the healing, nurturing life of the church. There are between three and five million at-risk kids with one or more of their parents in jail or prison. They are six times more likely to end up in prison themselves. These are the next generations' criminals who are at a loss unless we, the Church, begin to change our ministry strategies and incorporate Christian programs that will make a difference and have a great impact on our children with prevention as our focus.

We are passionate about saving America's youth by taking our message of "Generational Change" to schools and communities all across our country. We are also committed to working with Prison Fellowship Ministries on a project called "Operation Starting Line." It's a ministry event which enables professional Christian athletes, singers, musicians, comedians and speakers, like me, to reach the lost and minister in every prison in America.

We are putting into motion the words of Jesus. "I was in prison and you visited me" (Matthew 25:36) and "... in as much as you did it to one of the least of these, you did it to Me." (Matthew 25:40).

Prayer for Salvation

If you've never asked the Lord Jesus into your life, He is waiting with open arms.

There is no sin that the Father is not willing to forgive and forget. If you'll just ask Jesus to forgive you, He will. There is nothing more rewarding in life than to live for Him!

Pray this prayer now:

"Father God, I admit I'm a sinner, I believe that Jesus is the Son of God. I believe He died on the cross for my sins. I confess now with my mouth and believe in my heart that Jesus Christ was raised from the dead. I repent of all my sins. Jesus, I invite you now to be my Lord and Savior. I thank You Jesus for saving, delivering, and healing me; from this day on I will follow You. In Jesus' Name I pray, Amen."

If you prayed this prayer for the first time or recommitted your life to Christ, please tell someone. The Bible tells us, "If you publicly confess Jesus before others, He will confess you before His Father in Heaven."

Rocco Morelli
Ministries International

If you are led to help us in any way or would like us to share at your school, church, or event, please contact us at:

Rocco Morelli Ministries International
P.O. Box 135336
Clermont, FL 34713-5336
1-888-401-0367
E-mail: rcmorelli@rmministries.org
www.roccomorelli.org

The *World Reach Foundation* has been established for raising funds to take the life changing message of Jesus Christ to the schools, communities, churches, and prisons throughout the world. For more information about our foundation please go to our website, write, or call us.